Life Is Simple It's Just Not Easy

4 Keystone Traits To Live By

Written By

John Barrett

Published by

Rocket Publishing

ISBN: 0-9888284-7-2
ISBN-13: 13: 978-0-9888284-7-6

Published By: Rocket Publishing

Book Design By: John Barrett Art
www.johnbarrettart.com

Thanks:

My amazing wife, Erin, our two beautiful girls, Zion & Allie, and our little man, Isaiah. They teach me more about life than anyone else ever could. To everyone who helped bring this book together with their appreciated input. May you live life to the fullest, the way God intended.

CONTENT:

JohnBarrett
Faith | Leadership | Innovation

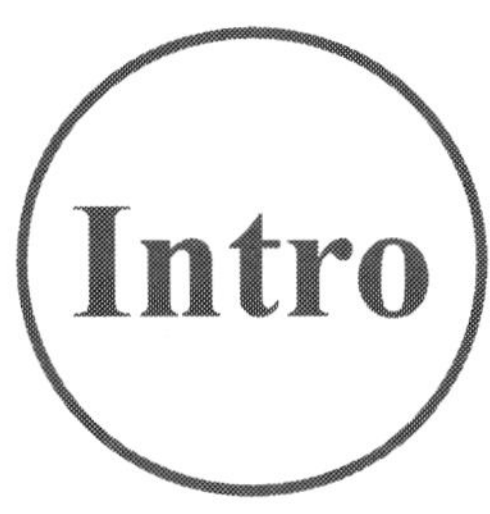

"I arise in the morning torn between a desire to improve the world and a desire to enjoy the world. This makes it difficult to plan the day."
~ E.B. White

I am going to die on Monday, February 13th, 2073—the day before my birthday. Yes, that's right; I am a Valentine's Day baby. Growing up, my mom called me Valentino. I call myself the love child. My wife says I am so full of love the universe couldn't help but celebrate me on February 14th. Anyway, back to my death…how do I know that I will kick the bucket the day before my birthday, you ask? Easy, I googled it and found a death clock. All I had to do was type in my stats, hit enter, and then wait for the giant countdown to pop up on my computer, showing me the exact time, to the millisecond, that I am going to die. There's nothing like seeing the countdown to your death on a big black screen to motivate—or depress—you. Thankfully, I chose the former.

Although the death clock is nothing more than a ridiculous joke, imagine if you could see your actual death clock countdown. What if every day you woke up to a read-out of your time left on Earth? I think we all might approach our days a little differently if we knew when our time was going to be up.

But why do we need a death countdown, or a near-death experience, to focus our attention on what matters? Why does it take, at best, an emotional movie or, at worst, a loved one's funeral to jolt us into realizing how precious life is?

If you are waiting for a life-altering situation to jump-start your heart, you are missing out on all that life has to offer right now. To get the most out of this life, we need to live with the daily knowledge that we have an expiration date. Moses' prayer, found in the Psalms, reflects his awareness of this sobering reality:

Psalm 90:12 (NIV)
Teach us to number our days, that we may gain a heart of wisdom.

In the old country song called *Live Like You Were Dying,* Tim McGraw encourages us to live life to the fullest with no regrets. The song received many accolades, including a Grammy Award for Song of the Year. Whether you like the song or not, it packs a powerful punch. We all need to awaken the desire inside us to make every day count. As followers of Christ, our inspiration to live like we are dying should be evident to all. We have received such a great salvation to live out with passionate determination.

Did you know the verb *inspire* means "to encourage somebody to greater effort, enthusiasm, or creativity: to awaken a particular feeling in somebody." It comes from the Latin word *inspirare* meaning "to breathe." God breathes passion into your spirit, awakening you to who you are called to be. This book is designed to inspire you to live every day with purpose, passion, and perseverance. I want to help awaken the God-given potential inside of you.

Do you ever feel like you're destined for so much more than you're currently experiencing? Like you haven't yet become all you're meant to be? Sure, some days, you're in the zone, doing exactly what you were created to do, but other days you feel like you're stuck in the mire of life. The truth is we all wrestle between these two realities. Why is it that some people find their way out of the muck and into the flow of purpose, while others can't seem to lift their feet out of the sludge? What if I told you that there is a way for you to live in the sweet spot of God's design? What if there were keystone traits to live by that could take your life to a whole new level? I have good news: there are!

There are two kinds of people in this life: those who grow and thrive and those who merely try to survive. I know you want to be counted among those who are thriving. That is why you are reading this book. Congratulations on taking the next step in your journey to living a victorious life! I have no doubt God will honor your commitment to become all He has planned for you. Charles M. Schwab said, "When a man has put a limit on what he will do, he has put a limit on what he can do."

As I sit here, writing in this coffee shop, there is a sign above my head which reads, "Behind every successful person there is a substantial amount of coffee." My Caramel Brûlée Latte and I agree. I like a good shot of espresso as much as the next person, and we have businessman Luigi Bezzera to thank for it; he was the inventor of espresso. It all started in 1903 while he was tinkering away with his coffee pot, trying to find a faster way to make coffee. Bezzera owned a manufacturing business and was frustrated by the time-consuming process of brewing his coffee at home each morning. He wanted a way to get quick, powerful shots of coffee for himself and his employees. Ultimately, he invented the espresso machine. Fast-forward in time, and now we can brew a high-powered espresso in seconds to get our caffeinated shot of energy. (No wonder people mistakenly pronounce it ex-presso, rather than es-presso.)

For many coffee lovers, the sign above my head rings true, but the real "stuff" behind a successful life is much more than coffee. The real stuff is a strong shot of Jesus. In the same way Bezzera created a high-powered shot of espresso, we need to be intentional about living a high-octane, Spirit-filled version of Christianity. We're not talking decaf here. Decaf coffee looks, smells, and even tastes somewhat like the real thing, but it doesn't have the strength to keep you going. In the same way, decaf Christianity misses the fullness of God's power for your life. God never intended for us to live the decaf life. His Spirit empowers us to live a high-octane adventure with Him. And His Word gives us specific instructions to maximize our experience here on Earth—keystone traits for us to live by.

As you read on, you are going to be challenged, encouraged, instructed, and inspired to start living your life to the fullest. What you read will spark your faith, enabling you to step into the unknown. You will find Scriptures and ideas that speak to you right where you are at on the journey. Perhaps you will be familiar with some of the concepts you read but realize you are not operating in them. This book will serve as the catalyst to get going again.

Whatever place you are in today, God is able to give you what you need right when you need it. My prayer is that this book will serve as His conduit to reach you with the truth you need to rise up and live. I ask that you commit to reading it in its entirety with a heart that seeks to hear from God. The right words at the right time produce the right outcome. Get ready to gulp four shots of high-powered keystone traits that will energize your spirit.

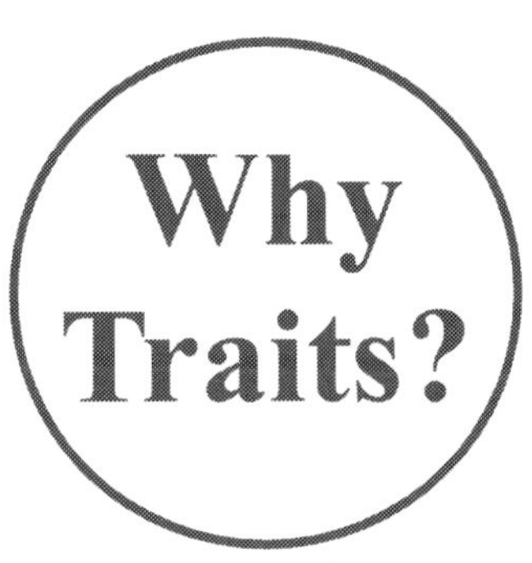

I enjoy playing golf, but I have to admit I am not very good at it. Knowing this, I have settled in my heart that my central purpose on the course is to provide comic relief in the midst of for an otherwise mentally taxing, high-stress game. It's not that I tell the best jokes; it's more that I am the joke. My rule when playing golf is to be as far from the ball after I hit it as I can. Usually, for me that looks like 10 feet on a drive and 100 feet on a putt—somehow I keep getting those mixed up!

Even though I can't play well, I do know that how you approach the ball and line up your feet with your body will determine how well you hit the ball. In golf, it is all about approach and alignment. In fact, you can't even expect to get a good swing at the ball if you aren't in the proper position.

In the same way, how well we swing and hit in life is, first and foremost, dependent on our approach. What do I mean by swinging and hitting? In the game of life, our perspective and attitude determine how far we'll go.

Proverbs 23:7 (NKJV)
For as he thinks in his heart, so is he.

If we are going to win in life, we have to understand how the game is played. To understand how the game of life is played, we have to understand how God created us and how we are uniquely designed to operate. God created us to function from the inside-out, not the outside-in. We are spiritual beings living in a physical reality. God's Spirit lives inside of us and works through us, shaping our behavior. It all starts on the inside and then flows out of us. What resides inside of you will guide your actions. If fear, doubt, and unbelief are in your heart, then you will act accordingly. If faith, trust, and hope are in your heart, then you will act according to those. People are not just a product of their circumstances; they are a product of their thinking. Author James Allen said, "You are today where your thoughts have brought you; you will be tomorrow where your thoughts take you." The way you approach life will be filtered through who you are—your traits.

"People are not just a product of their circumstances; they are a product of their thinking."

Traits are defined as distinguishing qualities or characteristics. They are the invisible attributes that make us who we are. Who we are ultimately determines what we do. Our internal being dictates our external doing. This explains why we are called human beings, not human doings. The German poet Johann Wolfgang Von Goethe said, "Before you can do something you must first be something." Our doing is the overflow of our being. Everything starts within us and then works its way out of us. The thoughts which develop inside our minds move us into action. Feelings, too, well up within us and influence our physical behaviors.

I'll give you a basic example of how this works. Think of a time when you started to cry during an emotional movie. As you watched the moving scene (good or bad) unfold, you were filled with emotion. Your limbic system (in the brain) sent a powerful neurotransmitter called acetylcholine to your lacrimal system (near the eyeball) that began to secrete an overwhelming amount of water. The tear ducts couldn't handle the volume, and the excess overflowed out of your eyes and streamed down your face, making you a sobbing mess during *The Notebook* (Men, you know you cried too; just admit it).

This simple example shows how what is inside of us always works its way out somehow. Make no mistake, our internal traits define who we are and what we'll eventually become. Greek Philosopher Heraclitus penned the Greek aphorism "Ethos anthropos daimon," which roughly translated states, "Character is a man's fate or destiny." Traits are the aspects of our character by which we subconsciously live. The Apostle Paul wrote, "Do not be deceived: God cannot be mocked. A man reaps what he sows." Your traits will define your life. What you sow on the inside will reap a harvest around you. This harvest will yield either a priceless treasure or a heap of trash, depending on what was planted. The sowing and reaping principle works regardless of what you put in. The traits you choose to live by mean the difference between caffeinated and decaf Christianity. Therefore, it is vital to meticulously develop the right traits.

Proverbs 4:23 (NCV)
Be careful what you think, because your thoughts run your life.

WHY KEYSTONE TRAITS?

Some traits are more important than others. These are called keystone traits, and they are essential to the successful life. They have the power to transform every area of your life.

Charles Duhigg, author of *The Power of Habit,* identified certain habits as "keystone habits." His research revealed that keystone habits are connected to other good habits. For example, exercising often goes hand-in-hand with better eating habits, and making your bed is linked to greater productivity. Duhigg writes, "Families who habitually eat dinner together seem to raise children with better homework skills, higher grades, greater emotional control, and more confidence."

Keystone habits cause a chain reaction which affects all your other habits. In the same way, the keystone traits you develop have the ability to transform your entire life. They govern your choices, impacting the way you approach your days. Kind of like the "one ring to rule them all" effect that J.R.R. Tolkien wrote about in *The Lord of the Rings* trilogy, there are certain traits that rule over all the rest. People who possess these keystone traits have the ability to harness God's principles and live life to the fullest. Keystone traits are specific character qualities that can change your future. When you get in alignment with the way God has called you to live, you will start to experience the destiny you were created for.

This book has taken me a lifetime to write. Not because it took that long to physically write, but because it took my whole life to identify which keystone traits are the most vital. I have experienced tremendous breakthroughs in my life as a result of being guided by the traits I am going to share with you. I have also endured challenging times which helped me to recognize the traits we need to hold onto in the midst of life's storms. These keystone traits are the embodiment of who we are designed to be. They make the difference between an empty existence and a fulfilling life.

By now, you're probably perched on the edge of your seat in anticipation of what these four, life-changing traits could be. I won't keep you in suspense any longer. The four keystone traits everyone must embrace to live successfully are hiding right in the word L.I.F.E.

LEADERSHIP

INTENTIONALITY

FAITH

ENTHUSIASM

Here is our working definition for each of the four traits:

***Leadership*:** The ability to believe in yourself, your purpose, and your skills to make a difference.

***Intentionality*:** The ability to develop a plan, do more than you don't, and discipline yourself to reach your potential.

***Faith*:** The ability to get complete trust in God, grow it, and give it to those who need it.

***Enthusiasm*:** The ability to always look for the good, laugh on the journey, and show love to all.

The good news is that God has hard-wired each of these traits within us, as creatures made in the image and likeness of God. We have all we need to be successful.

2 Peter 1:3 (NIV)
His divine power has given us everything we need for a godly life through our knowledge of Him who called us by His own glory and goodness.

This divine power within us must be activated by our belief in it. I believe that the fact you are reading this book is evidence of that. My prayer is that we will all embody these keystone traits and do what's necessary to live them out. Life is simple, it's just not easy.

Enjoy!

Keystone Trait

1 Leadership

2 Intentionality

3 Faith

4 Enthusiasm

Keystone Trait

1 Leadership

2 Intentionality

3 Faith

4 Enthusiasm

Keystone Trait

1

Leadership

Keystone Trait 1

LEADERSHIP

"Nothing so conclusively proves a man's ability to lead others as what he does from day to day to lead himself."
~ Thomas J. Watson

One of the most important traits needed for living a great life is leadership.

It's said that one day, Frederick the Great of Prussia was walking on the outskirts of Berlin when he encountered a very old man walking ramrod-straight in the opposite direction.
"Who are you?" Frederick asked his subject.
"I am a king," replied the old man.
"A king!" laughed Frederick. "Over what kingdom do you reign?"
"Over myself," the proud old man replied.

Most people think of leadership as a position of authority, but leadership begins much more humbly than that. Leadership begins by simply stepping up and taking responsibility. And the first person we are responsible for is ourselves. Think about the word responsible. It means to be response-able. Being responsible for self is being able to respond appropriately in any given situation. You are the one responsible for leading your life; no one can do it for you.

Unfortunately, you can't delegate your life to someone else. Wouldn't it be great if we could delegate our character to someone with remarkable character? How about delegating our need for compassion to someone who is full of compassion? What a relief it would be to delegate our faults to someone without fault! The reality is you can't delegate what you're responsible for. President Theodore Roosevelt once stated, "If you could kick the person in the pants responsible for most of your trouble, you wouldn't sit for a month."

You will never get the most out of life until you first learn to lead yourself. Let's dissect the word leadership: lead-er-ship… lead-ur-ship…lead-yur-ship…lead-your-ship (How'd you like that trick?). You have to lead your ship if you want to sail to great destinations. You are the captain of your soul, and God is the Commander. He gives you the orders, and it is your responsibility to carry them out with the help of the Holy Spirit. When we accept responsibility for the leadership of our own lives, we will begin taking those first steps toward greatness. Remember, leadership is more about who you are than what you do. It starts with an inward choice and becomes an outward expression.

"When we accept responsibility for the leadership of our own lives, we will begin taking those first steps toward greatness."

My drive for leadership is a defining force in my life. Most people attribute it to my love of entrepreneurial business strategies, but the real reason I am passionate about leadership is that I believe the quality of a person's life depends on their ability to lead themselves. I remember my desire as a young adult to learn all I could about leadership. I wasn't driven by the desire for position or power over others. No, my drive was birthed from a deep desire to lead myself and make a positive impact on the world. As I began to study and learn more about leadership, I discovered that it was more about me than the masses. I devoured any and every resource I could get my hands on to help guide my life.

During those young adult years, I didn't have the income, networking, know-how, or in some cases, the time machine needed to meet people like Norman Vincent Peale, Napoleon Hill, Dale Carnegie, C.S. Lewis, Dr. John C. Maxwell, A.W. Tozer, Ken Blanchard, and a host of others. So, I used the one resource I did have available to me: books. I even took a side job at a bookstore because I wanted to be surrounded by great ideas. I studied these leaders' resources and teachings, and it shaped my entire outlook on life.

I still remember listening to every Zig Ziglar tape (Yes, I said tape, as in cassette) as a young 20-year old working part-time as the janitor of a dialysis center in Maryville, Tennessee. I would clock in around midnight, pop in my Ziglar tape, and start cleaning. I listened to those tapes night after night until I had memorized every one of them. The dialysis center paid me to clean, but during those hours of cleaning, I was earning hundreds of credit hours towards a self-worth leadership degree. The principles I learned while cleaning that center directed the course of my career and inspired my devotion to personal development. Since that time, I have been on my own journey of leading prominent teams, organizations, and individuals down their path to leadership development. I was even able to write my first leadership book, *LEADOLOGY: 12 Ideas To Level Up Your Leadership*, because of these experiences, and it all started with the desire to first lead myself.

The most critical person anyone will ever lead is themselves. Forget leading others if you can't get a handle on your own life. Everyone, and I mean everyone, is called to be a leader by first conducting themselves well. If you can learn to believe in three things: yourself, your purpose, and your skills, you will begin to lead your life more effectively.

1.1

Believe In Yourself

Leadership

Believe In Yourself

The greatest obstacle you'll ever have to overcome is...yourself.

The hardest person you will ever battle is you and you alone. American writer Carl Sandberg once said, "There is an eagle in me that wants to soar, and there is a hippopotamus in me that wants to wallow in the mud." I think we can all relate to that statement. There are days when I am in the flow, and there are days when I can barely go. It's easy to believe in ourselves when we're in the flow, but the true test comes when we encounter obstacles along the road. It's in the midst of these challenging moments that we have to stay strong and keep moving forward despite the discouragement we feel. French-German theologian Albert Schweitzer said, "One who gains strength by overcoming obstacles possesses the only strength which can overcome adversity." If you think success comes without opposition, you have a faulty view of success. The road to success is filled with obstacles. My encouragement to you is to embrace the journey of life whatever comes your way and to keep on believing...you will get stronger. Mountaineer, explorer, and philanthropist Sir Edmund Hillary said, "It is not the mountain we conquer but ourselves."

There are three strategies we can practice that will help us believe in ourselves:

Think Well

The mind is the battlefield where war wages every day. If we give up the fight and surrender to our self-limiting beliefs, we will become the casualty of our worst thoughts. They will trap us in a prison of self-sabotaging distress. The Apostle Paul instructs us to "take captive every thought to make it obedient to Christ." Whatever thoughts go unchecked in our minds will become the reality we see in our lives.

> "Whatever thoughts go unchecked in our minds will become the reality we see in our lives."

How we think determines how we live. Our perception is oftentimes greater than our reality. We project our perceptions onto the world around us; they become the lens through which we view our circumstances. We don't see the world as it is, we see the world as we are. That is why beauty is in the eye of the beholder. Think about it. If we always think that people do not like us, then we will view every gesture people make toward us through the lens of rejection or judgment; if we are jealous of another person, then everything they acquire will irritate us. If we only see faults in others, we will judge and disapprove of every action they take.

However, if we have thoughts of peace towards others, no matter what they do, we'll live with grace for them. One of my favorite authors, James Allen, wrote, "To live continually in thoughts of ill will, cynicism, suspicion, and envy, is to be confined in a self-made prison hole. But to think well of all, to be cheerful with all, to patiently learn to find the good in all—such unselfish thoughts are the very portals of heaven; and to dwell day by day in thoughts of peace toward every creature will bring abounding peace to their possessor."

Because we see the world as we are, it is of utmost importance that we control our thoughts. If our thoughts get out of control, our lives will get out of control. If we think negative, depressing thoughts, we will become negative, depressing people. If we think joyful, fruitful thoughts, we will become joyful, fruitful people. Just like the expression "You are what you eat," so it is with our thoughts: "You are what you think." If you sabotage yourself by thinking negative thoughts, your life will become toxic with negativity. However, if you choose to build up an arsenal of positive thoughts from the truth of God's Word, then you will be charged up with the supernatural energy to accomplish what lies ahead.

Do you truly believe in yourself?

I want you to take a minute to think about that question. Do you really believe in yourself? Do you believe that you are capable of doing what you dream of doing and becoming who you were designed to become? I have found that most people believe God can do great things; they just don't believe God will use them to do those great things. To outperform your limiting beliefs, you have to gain self-confidence. If you don't value yourself as a child of God, you will never see value in what you do.

Philippians 4:8 (NIV)
Finally, brothers and sisters, whatever is true, whatever is noble, whatever is right, whatever is pure, whatever is lovely, whatever is admirable—if anything is excellent or praiseworthy—think about such things.

Change your thinking, and you will change your future. Challenge yourself to think thoughts that bear good fruit. Your thoughts will always take you somewhere; make sure it is where you are destined to go. Genuinely believe in yourself, and I guarantee you'll experience greater possibilities. Henry Ford said, "Whether you think you can or you think you can't, you're right."

Speak Well

The most important person you'll ever communicate with is yourself. What you say to yourself will determine the confidence you exude. The way you speak to yourself directs your path and determines your life. How you speak will define how you live. You can't speak failure over your life and expect to live successfully. If you consistently tell yourself that you are going to fail, there is a good chance you will.

Proverbs 11:17 (NKJV)
The merciful man does good for his own soul, but he who is cruel troubles his own flesh.

This isn't just positive mumbo-jumbo hype; it is how God created us. The brain is made up of billions of pathways through which information continuously travels. These pathways are constantly under construction. Neuroscientist' refer to this process as neuroplasticity. Basically, your brain is ever-adapting and reinventing itself based on the information it is receiving. As new pathways are paved, old ones break down.

This is either good news or terrible news, depending on what information your brain is currently processing. Environment, experiences, emotions, thoughts, and words have a tremendous impact on our ability to function optimally. This is how we learn new skills through regular practice. Our old pathways of depression, doubt, and chaos will begin to break down as we chart new pathways with productivity, positivity, and purpose. You, just by what you think and say to yourself, can literally rewire your brain. The messages you continually repeat to yourself become habitual pathways of activity in the brain.

Over time, your new thoughts and words will become your new actions and habits. What you communicate to yourself will wire your brain to produce a natural pathway to that result. If you continue to say and believe that you aren't a creative person, you will neurologically imbed that behavior. Your brain will struggle to foster creativity because it is blocked by the unimaginative pathway you have constructed. If you repeatedly tell yourself you don't have enough resources to get something done, your brain will have difficulty locating the resources to complete the task.

This is why we hit mental roadblocks when we do something we've never done before: our brain is breaking ground for the construction of a new pathway. If we surrender to an "I can't do it" attitude and give up in the midst of the struggle, the new pathway is abandoned and the brain will access the well-worn road of impossibility.

You must reject the idea that you are limited. The only limit you have is the belief that you have one. Don't trap yourself in a cage of uncertainty. Focus on what you can do and push past the roadblocks in your mind by speaking words of affirmation and encouragement to yourself. Envision who you want to become and speak like that version of yourself, not the person you currently are. Speak as though you can, and one day you will.

"Speak as though you can, and one day you will."

Matthew 12:33-37 (NKJV)
33 "Either make the tree good and its fruit good, or else make the tree bad and its fruit bad; for a tree is known by its fruit.
34 Brood of vipers! How can you, being evil, speak good things? For out of the abundance of the heart the mouth speaks.
35 A good man out of the good treasure of his heart brings forth good things, and an evil man out of the evil treasure brings forth evil things. 36 But I say to you that for every idle word men may speak, they will give account of it in the day of judgment. 37 For by your words you will be justified, and by your words you will be condemned."

Do Well

John Wesley said, "Do all the good you can, by all the means you can, in all the ways you can, in all the places you can, at all the times you can, to all the people you can, as long as ever you can." You'll never be more than you are right now if you don't do something you've never done before. It's not enough to talk about what you want to do. You have to be willing to step out in faith and do it. Take the leap from that comfortable nest of familiarity and fly into the unknown of possibility.

Isaiah 40:28-31 (NIV)
28 Do you not know? Have you not heard? The Lord is the everlasting God, the Creator of the ends of the earth. He will not grow tired or weary, and His understanding no one can fathom. 29 He gives strength to the weary and increases the power of the weak. 30 Even youths grow tired and weary, and young men stumble and fall; 31 but those who hope in the Lord will renew their strength. They will soar on wings like Eagles; they will run and not grow weary, they will walk and not be faint.

The bald eagle powerfully illustrates what it means to soar above and beyond the limits of the unknown. While other birds fly away from windy, even violent, conditions, the eagle meets the raging tempest head-on. Eagles fly into a storm, harness the power of the strong winds, and use this power to propel them above the turbulence and danger. We have to become like the eagle in order to overcome our fear of challenging conditions and the great unknown. Look beyond your self-imposed limits and find higher ground, just as the eagle does. No wonder Isaiah said God would mount us up on eagle's wings. He is giving us a picture of the life God has called us to, a life that soars against the storms. If we spend all of our time focusing on what could go wrong, we will miss the potential to see what could go right. Fear and worry have the ability to magnify themselves into an insurmountable size, and we succumb to them far too willingly.

Author Earl Nightingale once compared worry to a fog that can keep us from seeing things as they really are. He said, "A dense fog covering seven city blocks, to a depth of 100 feet, is composed of something less than one glass of water." You see, the fog of worry is an illusion that keeps us from our destiny. It is nothing for God to melt the mountains before us, and yet we fear the intangible "fog" that clouds our belief. We can live the overwhelmed life or the overcoming life. You were created to soar, so become an overcoming eagle and fly above your limiting beliefs.

REVIEW
KEYSTONE TRAIT 1
LEADERSHIP

(1.1) Believe In Yourself

a) Think Well
b) Speak Well
c) Do Well

1.2

Believe In Your Purpose

Leadership

Believe In Your Purpose

The most significant treasure a person can possess is the gift of purpose. Purpose gives us meaning and leads us to action.

One of the questions we all ask at different points in our lives is, "What is my purpose?" The question can overwhelm us, causing undue stress as we try desperately to discover our great purpose on the earth. If often feels like searching for a needle in a haystack.

Motivational speakers tell us, "Find your purpose!" We try and fail and try again…and fail. We hope it will simply drop into our lap, but it doesn't. We ponder the purpose question over and over and keep coming up empty. I believe there is more to life than finding one's purpose, though. I actually think that it is the wrong question to ask. I have found a much better question, one with a much more attainable answer. The better question to ask is, "Am I living with purpose?" We don't discover our purpose…we determine it.

> "We don't discover our purpose…we determine it."

No one discovers their purpose as though it is out there waiting for them somewhere. Purpose is something you create. You see, we were created with purpose.

We were designed for meaning. Everyone has purpose hard-wired within them from the beginning of time. Successful people live from a place of purpose, while the unsuccessful wait for it to magically appear. Purpose doesn't come upon us; it comes from within us. You get to determine what your unique purpose is, and you get to choose different purposes for different seasons and areas of life.

Joshua 24:15 (NIV)
But if serving the Lord seems undesirable to you, then choose for yourselves this day whom you will serve, whether the gods your ancestors served beyond the Euphrates, or the gods of the Amorites, in whose land you are living. But as for me and my household, we will serve the Lord.

"Purpose doesn't come upon us; it comes from within us."

Purpose looks different in every area of your life. You have a different purpose for your family than you do for your job. You have a different purpose for your health than you do for your finances. Life is filled with purpose of varying kinds. When you believe and operate in those purposes, you will be one step closer to living a successful life.

Here are three things to know about purpose:

Purpose Changes Your Perspective

I heard a great story about a wealthy father who took his son on a trip to the country so that the son could see how the poor lived. They spent a day and a night at the farm of an impoverished family. When they got back from their trip, the father asked his son, "How was the trip?"

“Very good, Dad!"

"Did you see how poor people can be?"

"Yeah!"

"And what did you learn?"

The son answered, "I saw that we have one dog at home, and they have four. We have a pool that reaches to the middle of the garden; they have a creek that has no end. We have imported lamps in the house; they have the stars. Our patio reaches to the front yard; they have the whole horizon." When the little boy finished, the father was speechless. His son then added, "Thanks for showing me how poor we are, Dad!”

Our focus gives us a proper perspective. With it, we can truly see the forest for the trees. Focus provides us with a God’s eye view of why we are doing what we are doing. Life’s challenges become blessings through the lens of meaning. We come to understand that challenges are not happening to us, they are happening for us.

2 Corinthians 5:7 (NIV)
For we live by faith, not by sight.

It’s much easier to endure when we know there is a light at the end of tunnel…and no it’s not a train heading our way for a collision. The light is the end to the testing of our faith in a challenging situation. When we see with the eyes of faith, we understand that everything is working towards our betterment. Instead of complaining about our circumstances, we can see that God is at work behind them. Though we may not fully understand why something is happening, we can trust that He will use it for our good.

Romans 8:28 (NIV)
And we know that in all things God works for the good of those who love Him, who have been called according to His purpose.

Purpose Changes What You Do

When you know what you are supposed to be doing, it's easier to identify whether or not you are doing the right thing. Purpose is an excellent filter for determining whether or not you are spending your time the right way. It is an internal compass helping us navigate our agendas. Don't go by a clock to determine your productivity, go by your purpose-driven compass. Our eternal perspective should direct our earthly objective. If how you are spending your time does not align with your purpose, you will need to abandon that pursuit. My mentor Dr. John C. Maxwell says, "You have to give up in order to go up."

We can't get preoccupied with temptations that pull us away from what we are created for. Too many people feel stuck doing what they don't want to do rather than freely living the life they were meant to live. Determining your purpose brings clarity to your daily duties. Every day should bring you one step closer to fulfilling your purpose. Jesus said He only did what He saw the Father doing. His internal purpose determined His external activity.

John 5:19 (NIV)
Jesus gave them this answer: "Very truly I tell you, the Son can do nothing by Himself; He can do only what He sees His Father doing, because whatever the Father does the Son also does.

We need to be very strategic and selective about how we invest our time. I have found that there are three types of people when it comes to time:

VICTIMS

These people are beat down and knocked out by their schedule. They cannot say no to anything or anyone, and their lives are cluttered with mere busyness. With no boundaries or defenses against the time stealers robbing them of their productivity, they over-schedule themselves with more than they can handle. Victims need to learn how to stand up and defend their time, or they will be destroyed by excessive commitments that aren't fulfilling their purpose.

MANAGERS

These people are barely keeping their heads above water as they tread back and forth. They are not getting ahead in life; they are simply maintaining what they have. Managers live on the brink of chaos. They focus on keeping the ship afloat, and spend most their time dumping out the excess water that keeps splashing onboard. These people deceive themselves by thinking that if they are managing their time, they are being productive, when the truth is they are not producing anything. They never have time to pursue their purpose because they are always dealing with the urgent demands of life, which suck up all their time and energy.

LEADERS

These people know how to make time work for them. They control their time; their time doesn't control them. They are focused what really matters and yield a fruitful harvest from their labor. They do not waste their time on urgent, or even good things. Instead, they commit their time to only those things that line up directly with their purpose—the best things. The rest they delegate to others, or they surrender them altogether. Leaders live with focus and purpose, doing what they are "called" to do.

Every day counts. Make the most of your day and aspire to be a leader of your time.

PURPOSE CHANGES OVER TIME

Ecclesiastes 3:1 (NJKV)
To everything there is a season, a time for every purpose under heaven...

We all have what I call seasonal purposes. These are the things that God has called us to do for the season we are in. Most things in life are seasonal. When the door of opportunity opens, we walk through it, receive our orders, and accomplish the task before moving on to whatever God has next for you. Purpose is not a one-stop destination. You don't spend your time striving to attain your purpose, only to think you are done once you find it. No, life is a series of seasonal purposes that God calls us to. Those seasons may be weeks, months, years, or even decades. The amount of time does not matter as much as identifying what we are called to do in each season of life and finishing it with excellence.

You may be in a season of growth, as God prepares you for future work. You may be in a season of doing the hard work. You may be coming to the end of a season. Whatever season you are in, be faithful to finish it. You will never move on to the next season of your life until you complete the one you are in. You can't skip seasons of purpose. You move from one to the next in God's perfect order. *You will never get out of your situation until you get what you need out of the situation.* I hope you got that last statement. Let me share it again just in case you missed it. *You will never get out of your situation until you get what you need out of the situation.*

Instead of praying to be released from a difficult season, start praying for a revelation of what God intends for you to glean from that season. Once you acquire the understanding or knowledge you need, you will be able to move on…but not until then. You are not entering a new season yet because there is still something for you where you are. Don't give up; keep digging for truth and freedom. Even reading this book at this particular time is part of the development process. Don't let the enemy steal the reward this season has for you by causing you to despair or lose focus. God is up to something, whether you can see it or not. He always has a purpose and a plan. He is training you and developing you for His next move in you. Get ready because God is preparing you for something great.

"You are not entering a new season yet because there is still something for you where you are."

Galatians 6:9 (NIV)
Let us not become weary in doing good, for at the proper time we will reap a harvest if we do not give up.

REVIEW

KEYSTONE TRAIT 1

LEADERSHIP

(1.1) Believe In Yourself

a) Think Well
b) Speak Well
c) Do Well

(1.2) Believe In Your Purpose

a) Purpose Changes Your Perspective
b) Purpose Changes What You Do
  - Victims
  - Managers
  - Leaders
c) Purpose Changes Over Time

1.3

Believe In Your Skills

Leadership

BELIEVE IN YOUR SKILLS

Years ago, my daughter asked me, "Daddy, do some people not have any talents?"

I quickly answered, "Everyone has talents."

She then responded, "Yeah, but some people might not have any talents, right?"

I said, "Baby, God has given everyone talents…everyone."

She asked again, "I know…but there have to be some people without talents…right?"

I responded again, "Everyone has talents. Besides, with God all things are possible, so anyone can have talents!"

She quickly said, "So, you're saying, if all things are possible, then it's possible that someone may not have any talents… right?"

I didn't know how to respond to her persistent line of reasoning. We all question our talents and gifts sometimes. Like my daughter, we just can't believe that we have what it takes to accomplish all that God has for us. We keep saying, "Yeah, but…" We believe other people are more gifted, more talented, or more intelligent than us. We overlook the significance of our abilities. We look at the external workings of everyone else's gifts and talents, but we too easily fail to see our own.

I cannot emphasize this truth enough: You have greatness within you. Yes, that's right. You have been created with a specific blend of gifts unique only to you. The most unfortunate people are those who live their whole lives without ever tapping into their gifts. Albert Schweitzer said, "The tragedy of life is what dies inside a man while he lives." You don't want to be like the gravestone that read, "Died at 30…buried at 90."

The greatest lie of the enemy is that you have nothing special to offer this world. It is the one lie that has kept multitudes of people trapped in chains of unworthiness. But it is *just a lie*. A lie can become a limiting belief if you let it. Or you can choose to believe the truth: God created you as His one-of-a-kind masterpiece. You are His handiwork, engineered for greatness. You have limitless potential because a limitless God created you.

1 Peter 4:10 (NIV)
Each of you should use whatever gift you have received to serve others, as faithful stewards of God's grace in its various forms.

In order to tap into this potential, you have to believe in your gifts. You have to believe that you have something special to offer this world. Most people do not recognize their own skills or talents because they come naturally to them. They think everyone else has the same knowledge or skill, too. However, it often happens that whatever you consider to be common knowledge is actually your particular area of gifting that God can use to bless or instruct others. Don't talk yourself out of sharing your gifts because you have believed the lie that you have nothing to offer.

Granted, you may find similarities between your skills and the skills of others, but they will never be identical. No one has the unique outlook and approach to life that you do. Don't belittle yourself by calling your gifts and skills common. You are extraordinary. Step out in faith and use your gifts to make a difference in the world. Don't let the limiting belief of sameness keep you from being unique.

2 Timothy 1:6-7 (NIV)
6 For this reason I remind you to fan into flame the gift of God, which is in you through the laying on of my hands. 7 For the Spirit God gave us does not make us timid, but gives us power, love and self-discipline.

> "Never make an internal agreement with your external adversary."

Fan your gifts into flame, trusting God to use them in a greater way. Don't let the enemy steal your future by making you believe that you are ineffective. Never make an internal agreement with your external adversary. He wants nothing more than to discourage you to the point of spiritual paralysis.

Here are four quick questions to help you identify your skills:

WHAT ARE YOU PASSIONATE ABOUT?

Purpose often unfolds when you identify a problem or frustration that needs to be resolved. The distinguishing characteristic, though, is your passion to enact change or improvement upon it. You will never bother to change something you aren't passionate about. The things you are passionate about grip you with an urgency that something must be done. These areas are usually tied into your skillset or gifting.

Another way to identify your passions is to reflect on what you read about, think about, or ask questions about. Also, consider what energizes you. Do you like to be in front of people or behind the scenes? Do you prefer to exert physical or mental energy? These insights will help you identify your true passion. Leonardo da Vinci said, "Where the spirit does not work with the hand, there is no art."

God's call on your life will always involve your predetermined passions. That's the reason why you gravitate toward certain areas of ministry but not others. Don't make it harder than it needs to be; simply look within to discover where your passions lie.

What Are Your Past Successes?

What tasks, events, programs, or opportunities have you excelled at? Success in a particular area can be an indicator of an individual's skill. It doesn't have to be a huge endeavor, just something that you have done well. If you can impact two people, you can impact 2,000 people.

Don't overlook the little things that you have accomplished for God. The little things we do well are significant indicators of what our skills are. When we're faithful with the small things, He will lead us to bigger things. King David was a shepherd long before he was a king. He had the skill of leading sheep. This season of his life ultimately prepared him to lead Israel. The defense tactics David learned to fight off bears and predators to protect the sheep were the tactics he later used to help the army of Israel become a military powerhouse.

Luke 16:10 (NLT)
If you are faithful in little things, you will be faithful in large ones. But if you are dishonest in little things, you won't be honest with greater responsibilities.

What Comes Easily To You?

We are naturally intuitive in our areas of skill or gifting. When you are able to learn a new skill quickly or accomplish assignments efficiently, that is an indicator of your strengths. What comes easily to you? What do you accomplish better or faster than anyone else? What is your subject of highest comprehension? In what area do you have that "gut feeling" which always seems to guide you in your decision making? Your unique gifts are hard-wired into your natural abilities. Many of the disciples were fisherman before Jesus called them to follow Him. Jesus said He would take their gifts and talents as fishermen and turn them into fishers of men. What was Jesus doing? He was shaping their man-made skills for His supernatural purposes.

What do people compliment you for? God uses people to affirm our skills and gifts. If you continue to hear the same remarks about how well you do something from various people, don't dismiss it. Sometimes we unintentionally overlook the skills we have even though they are obvious to everyone else.

What Do You Make Better?

When you are particularly skilled or gifted in an area, you will instinctively strive for excellence in it. Highly gifted individuals will take a project and improve it rather than diminish it. They tend to be more thorough in their execution than the average person. What do you do that only gets better when you work on it? What outcomes are more successful when you have worked on them? What projects meet a higher level of excellence when you are involved with them?

Your exceptional skills in a particular area will yield remarkable results and bring you favor with others. When you operate out of your strengths, your efforts will shine and you will be fruitful for the Kingdom. When we are following God's plan, we will always impact other people for their good and His glory.

It's time to live with purpose. Don't be hindered by limiting beliefs. Lead your life by believing in yourself, your purpose, and your skills.

REVIEW

KEYSTONE TRAIT 1

LEADERSHIP

(1.1) Believe In Yourself

a) Think Well
b) Speak Well
c) Do Well

(1.2) Believe In Your Purpose

a) Purpose Changes Your Perspective
b) Purpose Changes What You Do
- Victims
- Managers
- Leaders

c) Purpose Changes Over Time

(1.3) Believe In Your Skills

a) What Are You Passionate About?
b) What Are Your Past Successes?
c) What Comes Easily To You?
d) What Do You Make Better?

Keystone Trait

1 Leadership

2 Intentionality

3 Faith

4 Enthusiasm

Keystone Trait

2

Intentionality

Keystone Trait 2

Intentionality

"Our greatest fear should not be of failure but of succeeding at things in life that don't really matter."
~ Francis Chan

One day, little Johnny pulled out his bow and arrows to work on his target practice. Drawing the arrows out of his quiver one by one, he proceeded to shoot in whatever direction he felt like. He then walked up to wherever each arrow had landed and drew a target right around it, making it a bullseye every time.

Several arrows and targets later, his sister said, "You don't do target practice that way. You draw the target, then shoot the arrow."

Johnny responded, "I know that, but if you do it my way, you never miss!"

Unlike little Johnny, we can't just let our lives veer in any direction they want and draw a target around the place we end up. We need to maximize our potential by staying on the course of the lives we are called to live. We must be intentional about our direction and purpose. As the old saying goes, "We cannot direct the wind, but we can adjust our sails."

Spirituality requires intentionality. There are two ways to live: reactively or proactively. You can take life as it comes, or make it as you go. Unfortunately, most people just accept their lives as is, instead of intentionally leading them. They hope things will turn out better, but they don't put in the effort to actually make them better. Saying, "If God wants it done, He will do it," can easily become an excuse to be spiritually lazy. Our effort is significant in the eyes of God. He is looking for a good and faithful servant to whom He can say, "Well done."

> "Saying, 'If God wants it done, He will do it,' can easily become an excuse to be spiritually lazy."

Without intentionality, we can quickly get caught in the trap of unproductive busyness. Life becomes like an octopus on roller skates: lots of motion, but no progress. Scottish philosopher Thomas Carlyle said, "A person with a clear purpose will make progress on even the roughest road. A person with no purpose will make no progress on even the smoothest road." If we are not intentional about extracting the potential within us, we will miss the possibilities awaiting us. I have heard it said that potential is God's gift to us, and what we do with that potential is our gift back to Him. In the following parable, Jesus addresses living with intentionality.

Matthew 25:14-30 (NIV)
14 "Again, it (the Kingdom of Heaven) will be like a man going on a journey, who called his servants and entrusted his wealth to them. 15 To one he gave five bags of gold, to another two bags, and to another one bag, each according to his ability. Then he went on his journey. 16 The man who had received five bags of gold went at once and put his money to work and

gained five bags more. 17 So also, the one with two bags of
gold gained two more. 18 But the man who had received one
bag went off, dug a hole in the ground and hid his master's
money.
19 "After a long time the master of those servants returned and
settled accounts with them. 20 The man who had received five
bags of gold brought the other five. 'Master,' he said, 'you entrusted me with five bags of gold. See, I have gained five more.'
21 "His master replied, 'Well done, good and faithful servant!
You have been faithful with a few things; I will put you in
charge of many things. Come and share your master's happiness!'
22 "The man with two bags of gold also came. 'Master,' he
said, 'you entrusted me with two bags of gold; see, I have
gained two more.'
23 "His master replied, 'Well done, good and faithful servant!
You have been faithful with a few things; I will put you in
charge of many things. Come and share your master's happiness!'
24 "Then the man who had received one bag of gold came.
'Master,' he said, 'I knew that you are a hard man, harvesting
where you have not sown and gathering where you have not
scattered seed. 25 So I was afraid and went out and hid your
gold in the ground. See, here is what belongs to you.'
26 "His master replied, 'You wicked, lazy servant! So you knew
that I harvest where I have not sown and gather where I have
not scattered seed? 27 Well then, you should have put my money on deposit with the bankers, so that when I returned I would
have received it back with interest.
28 "'So take the bag of gold from him and give it to the one
who has ten bags. 29 For whoever has will be given more, and

they will have an abundance. Whoever does not have, even what they have will be taken from them. 30 And throw that worthless servant outside, into the darkness, where there will be weeping and gnashing of teeth.'

The two servants who chose to be proactive with the master's gift were rewarded. The one who buried it was rebuked. As you can see from this story, the choices we make today determine our tomorrow. We must intentionally commit to the destiny God has for us, knowing that we will always reap what we sow, whether good or bad. Coach John Wooden said, "There is a choice you have to make in everything you do. So keep in mind that in the end, the choice you make, makes you." The choices we make set us on the path we take. Whatever path we are on will lead us to its ultimate destination.

"The choices we make today determine our tomorrow."

Philippians 2:12b-13 (NIV)
12b...continue to work out your salvation with fear and trembling, 13 for it is God who works in you to will and to act in order to fulfill His good purpose.

We are called to "work out" our salvation. This means we are to steer our lives in the direction God intends. God will give us specific targets to shoot for in life as we faithfully pursue our potential.

There are three things you need to do if you want to live with intentionality: develop a plan, do more than you don't, and discipline yourself. Let's unpack these.

2.1

Develop A Plan

Intentionality

DEVELOP A PLAN

Reverend E. Paul Hovey said, "A blind man's world is bounded by the limits of his touch; an ignorant man's world by the limits of his knowledge: a great man's world by the limits of his vision."

Proverbs 29:18a (KJV)
Where there is no vision, the people perish...

Vision is only as powerful as its effect on people. Vision will push someone to work with a stronger sense of dedication and purpose. Without a vision for the future, it is difficult to live with intentionality.

> "When there is a sense of hope for the future, there is a surge of power in the present."

Christopher Wren, one of the greatest architects in London's history, was commissioned to build Saint Paul's Cathedral after the great fire of 1666. After observing three bricklayers working on a scaffold, Wren asked each man, "What are you doing?"
The first man who was crouched low to the ground replied, "Just making a living."

The second man, standing beside the first, said, "Just building a wall."
The third man, high on a ladder, working with noticeable dedication and determination said, "Creating a cathedral for the Almighty."

Indeed, the last man knew what his work was truly about; his vision was strong and clear. A clear vision is the first step to creating a detailed plan of action. The better you understand what you are working towards, the easier it is to develop a route to get there. Most people spend more time planning their grocery list than they do planning their lives. We have an innate desire for greatness, but to achieve it we first need vision. Then, in order to squeeze every ounce of potential from ourselves, we need to develop a game plan.

Proverbs 21:5 (ESV)
The plans of the diligent lead surely to abundance, but everyone who is hasty comes only to poverty.

> "The better you understand what you are working towards, the easier it is to develop a route to get there."

A few years ago, a friend and I were attending a conference in Atlanta, Georgia. We had spent the whole weekend immersed in learning and great conversation. We had worked diligently to feed our minds; however, in our eagerness to learn, we had forgotten to nourish our bodies, foregoing breakfast throughout the weekend. With our jam-packed schedule, by the last morning, we were starving.

As we started on the journey home, we knew what our first stop would be: breakfast. And no cheap fast food place was going to cut through this hunger. We wanted breakfast from a real restaurant, so we decided to find an IHOP. There was only one problem: we had no idea where the nearest IHOP was. We were determined, though; IHOP or bust. We asked SIRI, our personal iPhone tour guide, where the nearest IHOP was located. She assured us that it was only “a little ways from us.” Trusting her navigation, we drove around and around, following every navigational cue she gave us.

With IHOP just a few short turns away, we found ourselves in the middle of an upscale subdivision with an apparent minimum of four stories per home. Thinking we were about to eat at the fanciest IHOP we had ever seen, our anticipation grew and our stomachs growled even louder. Finally, we made our last turn before arriving at our final destination. We looked up, expecting to behold the Ritz-Carlton of IHOPS, and were shocked to find ourselves in the driveway of someone’s home.

There was no IHOP in sight. Actually, there were no restaurants at all in this upper-class residential neighborhood. We both looked at each other and realized that we had been had by SIRI! My friend and I had no clue where we were going, and as a result, we ended up nowhere. We did, however, get a friendly wave from the family staring at us through their window as they sipped their coffee. I considered asking if we could join them, but figured they might call the cops on us.

We never did find an IHOP, and we had to settle for fast food after all. We did learn an important lesson that day, though:

make sure you know where you are going if you want to arrive there.

We don't need SIRI or a GPS (Global Positioning System) to get where God wants us to go. He has given us His Holy Spirit, who leads us to our destiny, and He will never steer us wrong. He directs our internal guidance system and empowers us to accomplish His vision for our lives.

John 16:3 (NIV)
But when He, the Spirit of truth, comes, He will guide you into all the truth. He will not speak on His own; He will speak only what He hears, and He will tell you what is yet to come.

The Holy Spirit works to develop our internal guidance system. We don't need to look at the world to find our way; we need only look to the Spirit within us to navigate our future. In order to activate your navigation system and give the Holy Spirit your best attention and effort, you need to have what I call a spiritual G.P.S. (Goals, Persistence, and Sacrifice).

Goals

Zig Ziglar said, "If you aim at nothing, you will hit it every time." Goals are the targets we aim for and shoot at. They motivate us to keep moving forward; without them, it is easy to become complacent. Goals are God's way of keeping us in a growth mindset. If you do not know where you're supposed to end up, you will never reach your God-given destination.

Author Denis Waitley said, "The reason most people never reach their goals is that they don't define them, or ever seriously consider them as believable or achievable. Winners can tell you where they are going, what they plan to do along the way, and who will be sharing the adventure with them." It is vital that we set goals for every area of our lives. We should have goals for our family, finances, fitness, future, faith, and even our fun hobbies. Our goals should be forged through prayerful consideration and saturation in the Word. We need to set our goals based on where God is leading us. This is why it is imperative that we spend consistent time in the Word and in prayer to know Him and recognize His voice when He speaks to us about our next season of purpose.

When establishing your goals, it is important to be specific. How will you know when you've reached your goal if you cannot identify exactly what it is? For example, instead of saying, "My goal is to read more," indicate how many books you will read this year or how much time per day you will set aside each day to read. Instead of saying, "My goal is to be more caring," decide on specific actions you will take or projects you will get involved with to care for others. Instead of saying, "My goal is to be more generous this year," identify a specific amount of money you want to earn or set aside to give to certain people or causes. Your goals should be time-specific with measurable results.

The Holy Spirit will prompt you to establish the right goals for your life. He may not lay out the whole plan ahead of time (that's where faith comes in to play), but He does lead us step by step to the finish line.

Spend some time in prayer, asking God to show you what goals you should be working on and write them down.

Proverbs 16:3 (NLT)
Commit your actions to the Lord, and your plans will succeed.

Persistence

As I mentioned earlier, the road to success is paved with obstacles. As you identify and move toward the vision God has for your life, you are going to face roadblocks and detours along the way. It will take perseverance and commitment to make it to the mountaintop of success. If you only climb when you "feel like it," you will never reach new heights in life. Your initial excitement will wear off as the path grows steeper and rockier, and you will have to dig in and work hard, enduring to the end. But know that reaching the pinnacle of God's will for your life is worth every challenging step along the way.

> "If we only travel the familiar paths, we will never find the hidden treasures."

James 1:2-4 (NIV)
2 Consider it pure joy, my brothers and sisters, whenever you face trials of many kinds, 3 because you know that the testing of your faith produces perseverance. 4 Let perseverance finish its work so that you may be mature and complete, not lacking anything.

"Really? Consider it pure joy when I face trials. Why in the world do I do that?" you might be asking. Because you know that the tests you face and the process of persevering through them matures you until you are complete, not lacking anything.

I don't know about you, but I love the idea of being complete, a finished product. And, we don't do it alone. As the Apostle Peter said, "His divine power has given us everything we need for a godly life through our knowledge of Him who called us by His own glory and goodness."

When faced with obstacles and problems, it is easy to want to give up, but in order to reach your destiny, you have to fight through those setbacks and unforeseen challenges. The resistance you face is not necessarily a bad sign; it is often a sign that you are on the right path. So, shake off the dust and get back up. Remember this: you cannot climb a smooth mountain. It is the uneven, jagged, and rocky places that create the hand and foot holds you need to reach the top. When it seems like there is no way, remember what Thomas Edison said: "When you have exhausted all possibilities, remember this—you haven't." When the climb is steep and you're afraid to go on, ask the Holy Spirit for His strength and guidance to find your next step.

Ephesians 5:18 (NIV)
Do not get drunk on wine, which leads to debauchery. Instead, be filled with the Spirit,

Greek scholars note that the Greek present imperative tense is used for the words be filled. It has the implication of an ongoing replenishment, not a one-time occurrence. Truly, when we are filled anew each day with the Spirit, we can successfully persist through the greatest of challenges.

SACRIFICE

Author André Gide said, "You cannot discover new oceans unless you have the courage to lose sight of the shore." You will have to sacrifice your sense of comfort in order to fulfill your purpose. Whenever we are courageous enough to step outside of our comfort zone into the unknown, we have the potential to discover new areas of opportunity.

My wife and I had to make our purpose greater than our comfort years ago when we took a position out-of-state that resulted in a pay-decrease. We felt that, in order to fulfill what God had put in our hearts, the purpose was greater than the money. We knew that in order to experience God's provision and allow Him to use us, we were going to have to make this sacrifice. Even though our finances decreased, our purpose and growth increased! What we experienced in that season of our life was worth more than any amount of money we could have earned. Our financial comfort paled in comparison to the spiritual impact we were called to make. That test of sacrifice strengthened our faith.

Our comfort zones are bordered by familiarity. To step into the faith zone, we have to get uncomfortable and enter unfamiliar territory. Sure, it would be a relief to know everything in life before it happened, but it would also make life pretty boring and predictable. Get excited for something new…and better! My 17-year-old nephew was thinking about who he would ask to the prom when a pretty girl approached him at school and said, "Hey, if you were to ask me to prom, I wouldn't say no."

The rest is history.

Life would be so much easier if we could know the outcome before we had to step out and take a risk. Even though 20/20 foresight would be infinitely better than 20/20 hindsight, we do not have to live under the control of fear. Envision a life without fear of the unknown. Imagine being free to trust that whatever you are called to do, you know you'll have the God-given ability to achieve it. This is the faith it takes to live without limits. Let your faith become greater than your fears. God will never call you to something you can't accomplish with His help. We have one life to live, so live it to the fullest. Step out beyond your greatest fears and into a great faith adventure! Allow God to stretch you like a rubber band. The further you pull a rubber band back on your finger, the further it will fly when you let it go. We need to be stretched so that we can soar high into our destiny.

Hebrews 13:16 (NIV)
And do not forget to do good and to share with others, for with such sacrifices God is pleased.

REVIEW

KEYSTONE TRAIT 2

INTENTIONALITY

(2.1) Develop A Plan

a) Goals
b) Persistence
c) Sacrifice

2.2

Do More Than You Don't

Intentionality

Do More Than You Don't

For many years, Bronnie Ware worked in palliative care. Her patients were those who had gone home to die in the comfort of their familiar surroundings. She was able to witness some incredibly special moments while caring for them during the last three to twelve weeks of their lives. She ended up writing an insightful book about her experiences called, *The 5 Regrets of the Dying*. Here are the top five regrets as explained in her book:

#5 – "I wish that I had let myself be happier."
#4 – "I wish I had stayed in touch with my friends."
#3 – "I wish I'd had the courage to express my feelings."
#2 – "I wish I hadn't worked so hard."
#1 – "I wish I'd had the courage to live a life true to myself, not the life others expected of me."

What a powerful statement: "I wish I'd had the courage to live a life true to myself." These insights remind me of what Mark Twain once said: "Twenty years from now you will be more disappointed by the things that you didn't do than by the ones you did do. So throw off the bowlines. Sail away from the safe harbor. Catch the trade winds in your sails. Explore. Dream. Discover."

Are you a Do-er or a Don't-er? Do-ers are people of action; Don't-ers are people of apathy. It's the Do-ers who experience life to the fullest, while the Don't-ers experience lives of emptiness.

James 1:22 (NIV)
But be doers of the word, and not hearers only, deceiving yourselves.

To live a life of intentionality, you must have an extreme bias toward action—the drive to make your life count. The good thing is that, in my opinion, everyone possesses this desire; it's just a matter of extracting and activating it. The goal of life is not to arrive at death safely, but sparingly. By sparingly, I mean to live fully and to die empty. To have poured out your life with abandon, having nothing left to give at the end. Life is too short to live with could have, should have, would have regrets. Do-ers hold nothing back. They live out their faith rather than living in fear. This is why the book of Acts is not called the book of Ideas… it's about people who acted on their faith and did what God called them to do, making no excuses. Author Mark Batterson wrote, "At the end of your life your greatest regrets will not be the things you did but wish you hadn't, but it will be the things you didn't do but wish you had."

"Life is too short to live with could have, should have, would have regrets."

Proverbs 20:4 (NIV)
Sluggards do not plow in season; so at harvest time they look but find nothing.

Here are some of the different characteristics that show the difference between Do-ers & Don't-ers:

DO-ERS ASK, "HOW CAN IT BE DONE?"
DON'T-ERS ASK, "CAN IT BE DONE?"

Ronald Reagan had a sign that simply read, "It Can Be Done." This sign, sitting on his Oval Office desk, was Reagan's constant reminder that great and impossible things were within his grasp. Reagan came into office on the platform of three basic tenets: defeating Communism, cutting taxes, and shrinking the size of government. While he will be celebrated for his leadership and strength in these areas, history will also show that one of his greatest achievements was the revitalization of the American spirit and the cultivation of American pride. When I was growing up, I remember a popular expression used in the education system that said, "Where there's a will, there's a way." This was based on the idea, just like the President's sign, that there is always a way. Remember, our God is the God of the impossible.

Matthew 19:26 (NIV)
Jesus looked at them and said, "With man this is impossible, but with God all things are possible."

Are you a Do-er or a Don't-er?

- Don't-ers ask, "Can I?"
- Do-ers ask, "How Can I?"

There is a world of difference between these two approaches to life. Don't-ers always question their potential and ability. They get caught in a vortex of insecurity, causing them to live a decaf Christian life. In contrast, Do-ers are caffeinated Christians who rise to challenges and reach for greater opportunities, stepping out in faith to meet them. Don't-ers are mired in doubt, asking the question, "Can I?" while the Do-ers forge ahead, eager to figure out, "How can I?" They learn as they do. Author Ray Bradbury got it right when he stated, "Jump off the cliff and build your wings on the way down."

Philippians 4:13 (NIV)
I can do all things through Christ who strengthens me.

Notice the Apostle Paul said, "I can..." He didn't say, "I might be able to..." He didn't say, "One day, I hope to..." He was convinced of his empowerment. We need to have the same kind of resolve in our faith. Don't be a thermometer who simply reflects the temperature of its surroundings. Be a thermostat and set a new temperature for your future. God has empowered us to be agents of change, not victims of our circumstances. Don't focus on if you can do it; focus on how God's going to use you to do it.

Do-ers Embrace Experiences
Don't-ers Embrace Excuses

Life is a series of experiences which can shape and teach us for our betterment if we allow them to. Do-ers embrace the life lessons they learn from every encounter...good or bad. They see experiences as a stepping stone to the refinement of their character and are willing to take risks as a result. They are not afraid to make mistakes, because they understand that the road to success is paved with failures. Do-ers see themselves as students who are always learning and growing into greater potential.

Proverbs 18:15 (NLT)
Intelligent people are always ready to learn. Their ears are open for knowledge.

Don't-ers see opportunities as a pass/fail endeavor. The event has greater significance than the experience. They perceive any type of failure as fatal to their future. They don't see the growth opportunity embedded in the failure; they only see the failure itself. Past experiences cause them to fear mistakes, and then they make excuses to talk themselves out of stepping out again. These excuses seem rational to them because the end goal of a Don't-er is to avoid the pain of their worst fear—failure. But excuses are just lies in disguise. They keep people from their potential and their ultimate destiny. Don't-ers will come up with every reason why they can't do something. Their self-limiting fears keep them from opening themselves up to new opportunities.

"Excuses are just lies in disguise."

As followers of Christ, we are called to believe big and risk much. Embrace experiences and acquire knowledge. Don't be a critic, be a student. Critics are always looking for what's wrong, but students are always seeking a chance to learn and grow. The famous poet T.S. Eliot said, "Only those who will risk going too far can possibly find out how far one can go."

Do-ers are Decisive
Don't-ers are Distracted

To live life with intentionality you must be decisive. Indecisiveness prevents action and kills opportunity. Analyzing every detail stalls forward progress. William Arthur Ward said, "The optimist lives on the peninsula of infinite possibilities; the pessimist is stranded on the island of perpetual indecision." Many people are stuck in the paralysis of analysis. They are drowning in a sea of distractions. We are not called to be a Las Vegas odds calculating analyst. We are called to be faith-filled, risk-taking, obedient disciples of Jesus. But it is very difficult to be decisive when we are preoccupied with trying to figure out every reaction to our actions before we make a move. I am not saying we should act hastily, but most of us make excuses and talk ourselves out of acting altogether. In the following passage, we see how the Apostle Peter took decisive action requiring bold faith which resulted in the impossible becoming possible.

> "Indecisiveness prevents action and kills opportunity."

Matthew 14:22-32 (NIV)

22 Immediately Jesus made the disciples get into the boat and go on ahead of Him to the other side, while He dismissed the crowd. 23 After He had dismissed them, He went up on a mountainside by Himself to pray. Later that night, He was there alone, 24 and the boat was already a considerable distance from land, buffeted by the waves because the wind was against it.

25 Shortly before dawn Jesus went out to them, walking on the
lake. 26 When the disciples saw Him walking on the lake, they
were terrified. "It's a ghost," they said, and cried out in fear.
27 But Jesus immediately said to them: "Take courage! It is I.
Don't be afraid."
28 "Lord, if it's you," Peter replied, "tell me to come to you on
the water."
29 "Come," He said.
Then Peter got down out of the boat, walked on the water and
came toward Jesus. 30 But when he saw the wind, he was
afraid and, beginning to sink, cried out, "Lord, save me!"
31 Immediately Jesus reached out His hand and caught him.
"You of little faith," He said, "why did you doubt?"
32 And when they climbed into the boat, the wind died down.
33 Then those who were in the boat worshiped Him, saying,
"Truly you are the Son of God."

Jesus didn't tell Peter to mull over every detail and calculate every risk that could come along with stepping out of the boat and walking on water. He just said, "Come." Like Peter, we don't always know how it's going to work, but that should never keep us from trusting God's plan. We won't always know how God's plans are going to work on the front end of faith. Remember, 2/3rd's of God's name is GO. Notice that Peter was in good shape until he took his eyes off Jesus. He got distracted by the circumstances, and his faith faltered. Distractions breed doubt. Doubt breeds discouragement. And discouragement breeds faithlessness.

The word distraction means to be pulled apart. The word depicts a medieval method of torture where people were torn apart at the seams of their limbs, by being tied to four horses going in opposite directions. This became known as "death by dis-traction." We cannot allow our faith to become distracted from the destiny God has set before us. Everyone is tempted by distractions every day. The key is to put our spiritual blinders on and keep moving forward.

REVIEW

KEYSTONE TRAIT 2

INTENTIONALITY

(2.1) Develop A Plan

a) Goals
b) Persistence
c) Sacrifice

(2.2) Do More Than You Don't

a) Do-ers Ask, "How It Be Done?"
Don't-ers Ask, "Can It Be Done?"
b) Do-ers Embrace Experiences
Don't-ers Embrace Excuses
c) Do-ers Are Decisive
Don't-ers Are Distracted

2.3

Discipline Yourself

Intentionality

DISCIPLINE YOURSELF

It's not what we don't know that holds us back; it's what we know, but don't do, that holds us back. The greatest gap we will ever face in life is between knowing and doing. It is what separates the Do-ers from the Don't-ers. It is what keeps people from experiencing breakthroughs in their lives. It is the great divide that very few can bridge. Everyone knows how to lose weight, but how many actually do what is necessary to eat right and exercise? Everyone knows how to save money, but how many deny themselves immediate gratification for future opportunities? Everyone knows how to be more courageous, but how many step out of their comfort zones? The key characteristic of those who successfully bridge the divide between knowing and doing is discipline.

> "It's not what we don't know that holds us back; it's what we know, but don't do, that holds us back."

Discipline is the bridge between what you know and where you want to go. Here is our working definition of discipline: Discipline is the means by which you get what you really want, even when you don't want to do the thing necessary to get it.

Do not be plagued by the Law of Diminishing Intent, which says, "The longer you wait to do something you should do now, the greater the odds are you will never actually do it." Zig Ziglar looked at it this way: "If you do what you need to do when you need to do it, then the day will come when you can do what you want to do when you want to do it." Discipline requires willpower. And willpower is a muscle; the more you use it, the bigger it gets.

As I mentioned earlier, Charles Duhigg, author of The Power of Habit, extensively researched how having the willpower to change one keystone habit can affect all our other habits. Duhigg said, "As people strengthened their willpower muscles in one part of their lives—in the gym, or a money management program—that strength spilled over into what they ate or how hard they worked. Once willpower became stronger, it touched everything." The results show that the more you use your willpower to change your outcome, the more it will affect every area of your life for the good.

Your level of discipline will grow when these three things are happening in your life:

YOUR WHY IS GREATER THAN YOUR WHY NOT

If you want to be disciplined, you have to have a strong why. We only modify our behavior when the pain of staying the same is greater than the pain of changing. When your why is compelling, it creates a pathway of discipline. We only change our behavior when our fundamental belief about our behavior changes. The benefit of changing must surpass the comfort of staying. Discipline is hard. I read a meme on Facebook the other day that stated: "Losing weight is hard, being overweight is hard…choose your hard." Being intentional is not an easy feat, but the payoff is huge.

But, the truth is none of us wakes up desiring to take the harder road. The human brain is designed to take the path of least resistance. It seeks the simplest, most non-confrontational approach to life. For example, it is scientifically proven that our brains are always trying to find a way to burn as little calories as possible in an effort of self-preservation. In this way, taking the path of least resistance is not necessarily a bad thing; it can be a means of survival.

In order to concentrate, your brain is wired to focus on only what it absolutely needs to focus on. This is why you have voluntary and involuntary actions. It's necessary for your brain to think through how your hands need to move as you type on a keyboard, but you don't have to think about your heart beating in order to keep your blood pumping. Your body automatically does that without you having to consciously think about it. Likewise, you don't have to tell your body to breathe in order to keep yourself from suffocating. Your brain eliminates the need for you to consciously think about these involuntary actions so that your mental energy is reserved to focus on other voluntary tasks.

There are times, however, when thinking with a path of least resistance mindset can stunt your growth. Because we are excuse-filled beings who always try to take the easy route, we have to train our brains so that they don't backfire on us. In order to live life to the fullest, we can't let our brains do whatever they want; we have to transform them to operate in a way that moves us from surviving mode to thriving mode—and this takes intentionality.

Romans 12:2 (NIV)
Do not conform to the pattern of this world, but be transformed by the renewing of your mind.

> "You'll be successful when your dreams are bigger than your excuses."

Telling yourself that you can do something will cause your brain to work on figuring out how to make it a reality. In the same way, if you tell yourself you can't do something, your brain will go to work figuring out every excuse to make that belief a reality, too. When you eliminate your excuses, you liberate your potential. Transform what you tell yourself and you'll transform what you can do. You'll be successful when your dreams are bigger than your excuses. Your why has to be bigger than your why not. If you lose your why, you'll lose your way.

YOUR FIFO IS GREATER THAN YOUR FOMO

FOMO (Fear Of Missing Out) is a cultural buzzword of the day. Our society is plagued with people who feel like they are on the outside looking in. With everyone posting highlight reels of their best moments on social media, there are many who are becoming unnecessarily discouraged as they compare their real, everyday lives with the glorified highlights of others. FOMO can cause people to make rash decisions in their quest to live like the Joneses. Coveting what they see in others' lives leads them to run after things they were never meant to have. It can also cause them to stop dead in their tracks, caught in the trap of comparison, leaving them with feelings of worthlessness and hopelessness. In either case, FOMO is an anxiety-inducing stressor which leads to poor decision making.

Rather than suffering from FOMO, people need to be guided by what I call "FIFO": Faith In Future Opportunities. You activate self-discipline when you believe there is something better in the future than what you are experiencing in the present. People with a strong sense of FIFO will pay now in order to play later. They see the future with optimism and hope. This helps them to deny their desire for instant gratification in favor of future greatness. French poet Victor Hugo said, "The future has several names. For the weak, it is impossible; for the fainthearted, it is unknown; but for the valiant, it is ideal."

Throughout the '60s and '70s, Walter Mischel conducted testing at Stanford University which became known as the Marshmallow Test. Children were put in a room by themselves with one single marshmallow. They were told they could choose to either eat the marshmallow immediately or wait for an extended amount of time and receive more marshmallows. Only three out of ten children could resist the urge to eat the marshmallow instantly. What's fascinating are the findings that came 30 years after the study was completed, when further research was conducted on these same test subjects (now adults).

They discovered that the "Delayers" were predominately more successful in life overall. The "Non-Delayers" were 30% more likely to be overweight, suffer from drug addictions, and have a record of criminal activity. Psychologists call this phenomenon Hyperbolic Discount: the farther away a reward is in the future, the less motivation there is to achieve it. But when your FIFO is greater than your FOMO, you are motivated to endure even through insurmountable odds. Something invigorating happens to us when we live with expectancy and patience for the future. When we have a sense of hope for the future, there is a surge of power in the present. Those whose FIFO is greater than their FOMO will increase their level of discipline now to become more successful down the road.

2 Corinthians 4:17-18 (NIV)
17 For our light and momentary troubles are achieving for us an eternal glory that far outweighs them all. 18 So we fix our eyes not on what is seen, but on what is unseen, since what is seen is temporary, but what is unseen is eternal.

YOUR COMMITMENT IS GREATER THAN YOUR CIRCUMSTANCE

Inner commitments create external guardrails. Your core values act like a rudder for your decisions. When you pre-commit to a certain behavior, it is much easier to discipline yourself to follow through in the moment. Being prepared for what lies ahead empowers you to be successful when you get there. I like how boxer Joe Frazier put it: "You can map out a fight plan or a life plan, but when the action starts, it may not go the way you planned, and you're down to your reflexes—that means your preparation. That's where your road-work shows. If you cheated on that in the dark of the morning, well, you're going to get found out now, under the bright lights."

The secret to making good choices is to make the choice before you have to make the choice. Commitment on the front end helps you follow through on the back end. Deciding to live by faith before challenging circumstances arrive in your life will prepare you to live victoriously when you encounter them.

> "The secret to making good choices is to make the choice before you have to make the choice."

When you give yourself an, "If this happens, then I will..." type of commitment, it can keep you in the lane of discipline. For example, if you are trying to lose weight and have been invited to a party where the desserts served will be a temptation, then you can make the decision beforehand how to respond to that situation. "If I am offered dessert, then I will politely decline and drink a glass of water instead." Or, if you are going shopping, you could predetermine the amount you will spend. "If I see something over my allotted budget, then I will not purchase it until I save the money in cash."

It works with relationships, too. If you are going to be in the company of someone who has exhibited a pattern of making hurtful comments, you can decide beforehand how you will handle that inevitability. "If Jane intentionally or unintentionally puts me down, then I will choose to forgive her and free myself from her comment." Deciding to walk in forgiveness before someone hurts you prepares you to respond with humility rather than having a knee-jerk reaction in the moment. Don't spend today repairing yesterday's mistakes. Take time today to prepare for tomorrow. Make the internal decisions now that will guide your outward activity later. British Prime Minister Benjamin Disraeli said, "The secret of success in life is for a man to be ready for his opportunity when it comes."

Psalm 37:5 (NKJV)
Commit your way to the Lord, trust also in Him, and He shall bring it to pass.

REVIEW

KEYSTONE TRAIT 2

INTENTIONALITY

(2.1) Develop A Plan

a) Goals
b) Persistence
c) Sacrifice

(2.2) Do More Than You Don't

a) Do-ers Ask, "How It Be Done?"
Don't-ers Ask, "Can It Be Done?"
b) Do-ers Embrace Experiences
Don't-ers Embrace Excuses
c) Do-ers Are Decisive
Don't-ers Are Distracted

(2.3) Discipline Yourself

a) Your Why Is Greater Than Your Why Not
b) Your FIFO Is Greater Than Your FOMO
c) Your Commitment Is Greater Than Your Circumstance

Keystone Trait

1 Leadership

2 Intentionality

3 Faith

4 Enthusiasm

Keystone Trait

3

Faith

KEYSTONE TRAIT

FAITH

"The Christian faith is a grand cathedral, with divinely pictured windows. Standing without, you can see no glory, nor can imagine any, but standing within every ray of light reveals a harmony of unspeakable splendors."

~ Nathaniel Hawthorne

> "Faith is the lens through which we see God."

Faith is the currency of God's Kingdom. It's the means by which we experience the fullness of God and the hinge that opens the windows of Heaven. One cannot truly know God unless they possess a measure of faith. We must fundamentally understand that faith is the lens through which we see God—it brings our destiny into focus. C.S. Lewis said, "I believe in Christianity as I believe that the sun has risen: not only because I see it, but because by it I see everything else." If there is no need for faith on your journey, you're on the wrong journey.

Hebrews 11:6 (NIV)

And without faith it is impossible to please God, because anyone who comes to Him must believe that He exists and that He rewards those who earnestly seek Him.

Just as a house needs a strong foundation to build upon, our future must be built upon faith's firm foundation. The stronger our faith, the higher we can build. When our life is built upon Christ, the Solid Rock, we can withstand the storms of life and grow into the fullness of our destiny. Jesus shared this great parable to help us understand what faith is all about:

Matthew 7:24-27 (NIV)
24 "Therefore everyone who hears these words of mine and puts them into practice is like a wise man who built his house on the rock. 25 The rain came down, the streams rose, and the winds blew and beat against that house; yet it did not fall, because it had its foundation on the rock. 26 But everyone who hears these words of mine and does not put them into practice is like a foolish man who built his house on sand. 27 The rain came down, the streams rose, and the winds blew and beat against that house, and it fell with a great crash."

Notice that both the wise man and the foolish man faced hardship. They were both subjected to the same rain, flood, and wind. Just because one was wise didn't mean that he was free from difficulty. Too many times we think that if we are following Christ, we won't ever face problems. There are even those who think something is wrong with them if they do face troubles. Jesus never promised those who followed Him a life exempt from trials. The wise and the foolish live and breathe in the same, broken world. Both face the same temptations and challenges in life. It is the one who builds his life on the Rock (whose faith is in Christ) who will stand firm when trouble comes. Trouble is inevitable; it is up to you to choose to stand firm and not be shaken. Author J. R. R. Tolkien said, "Faithless is he that says farewell when the road darkens."

A wise man's faith is not rooted in perfect circumstances; it is rooted in a perfect Savior. Too many times we are telling God about our circumstances when we need to be telling our circumstances about our God. God is not moved by our worries and complaints; He is moved by our faith. The Bible shows us that it is by faith that we experience God's provision.

Matthew 9:27-30a (NIV)
27 As Jesus went on from there, two blind men followed him, calling out, "Have mercy on us, Son of David!" 28 When he had gone indoors, the blind men came to him, and he asked them, "Do you believe that I am able to do this?" "Yes, Lord," they replied. 29 Then he touched their eyes and said, "According to your faith let it be done to you"; 30 and their sight was restored.

These two men's faith that made all the difference for their futures. Faith exceedingly fuels our hope in every situation. Jesus was not moved by these men's circumstances, but by their faith. He said, "According to your faith let it be done to you." It's not that faith changes your circumstances, but it does change you, thereby changing your ability to overcome your circumstances. When faith rises up within you, it begins to transform the things around you. You cannot live an adventurous life with an apathetic faith. Never let your fear of the unknown keep you from having faith in the unseen. When

"You cannot live an adventurous life with an apathetic faith."

we live with unwavering faith, we'll experience a victorious life.

There are three things we need to know about faith. We need to know how to get it, grow it, and give it.

3.1

Get Faith

GET FAITH

Faith…you gotta have it in order to use it.

You can't step out in faith if you don't have any. Faith doesn't magically appear in our lives. It is something that we acquire over time, with practice. Each one of us has a measure of faith; some greater, some smaller. The good news is that it only takes a little faith to see big results. Jesus referred to this in the Gospel of Matthew:

Matthew 17:20 (NIV)
"Truly I tell you, if you have faith as small as a mustard seed, you can say to this mountain, 'Move from here to there,' and it will move. Nothing will be impossible for you."

Notice, Jesus said, "You can say to this mountain…" He didn't say *He* would talk to the mountain; *we* are to talk to the mountain. Our faith moves mountains by either smashing them or scaling them. Faith says "I'm Possible" rather than "Impossible." It changes the core of who we are, altering the way we view and live life. You see things differently than you did before. It gives you a perspective of perseverance in the midst of obstacles. Saint Augustine said, "Faith is to believe what you do not see; the reward of this faith is to see what you believe." You know you have faith when your decisions are centralized around God's plan. It shifts your mindset from what you can do to what God can do through you.

"Our faith moves mountains by either smashing them or scaling them."

If faith is the key to experiencing the fullness of God's plans for our lives, how do we get it?

By Jesus

Faith isn't just about what you believe; it's about Who you believe in.

Hebrews 12:1-2 (NKJV)
1 Therefore we also, since we are surrounded by so great a cloud of witnesses, let us lay aside every weight, and the sin which so easily ensnares us, and let us run with endurance the race that is set before us, 2 looking unto Jesus, the author and finisher of our faith, who for the joy that was set before Him endured the cross, despising the shame, and has sat down at the right hand of the throne of God.

Jesus is the Author and Initiator of our faith. It is only by Him and through Him that we can attain a greater measure of faith. He is the embodiment of faith. James reminds us in his book that without faith it is impossible to please God, because anyone who comes to Him must believe that He exists. When we place our faith in Jesus, He plants faith in us.

Colossians 2:12 (NIV)
Having been buried with him in baptism, in which you were also raised with him through your faith in the working of God, who raised him from the dead.

When we put faith in Jesus, we get to see His power at work in our lives. We are made alive in Christ and faith is the outpouring of our belief in Him. You see, our faith is not in ourselves, but in the power of God. Our faithlessness is buried by belief, as our faith is resurrected in Jesus. It's not that we have faith in Jesus, it's that Jesus is our faith. It's He who lives in us, not ourselves.

Galatians 2:19-20 (NIV)
19 For through the law I died to the law so that I might live for God. 20 I have been crucified with Christ and I no longer live, but Christ lives in me. The life I now live in the body, I live by faith in the Son of God, who loved me and gave himself for me.

As believers, we no longer live; our lives are hidden in Christ. Our position isn't based on our condition; it is based on who we are in Christ. All things are possible not because of us, but because of Him. We get faith because we've got Jesus. He came to bring us the faith we need in order to live the life we should. True faith shifts the focus off of us and onto Jesus.

Galatians 3:23-25 (NIV)
23 Before the coming of this faith, we were held in custody under the law, locked up until the faith that was to come would be revealed. 24 So the law was our guardian until Christ came that

we might be justified by faith. 25 Now that this faith has come, we are no longer under a guardian.

By Hearing

Romans 10:17 (NKJV)
So then faith comes by hearing, and hearing by the word of God.

When I was in high school, we had a massive snowstorm two weeks before Christmas break, which resulted in a total of four weeks off school! As a teenager, this seemed like a dream come true, but I quickly realized that, with all the roads and business shut down, there wasn't much to do.

One of those snowy nights, I remember sitting in my bedroom and spotting my Bible. Feeling guilty that I hadn't been reading it much at all, I picked it up and crawled into bed. What I thought was going to be a quick peace offering for my shame, turned out to nearly become an all-night reading marathon. I couldn't put the Bible down! As I was reading, I kept highlighting these amazing passages that were speaking to my heart. Over that extended break, I read almost the entire New Testament. It changed me. To this day, I credit a big part of my faith foundation to that four-week experience. It paved the path for faith to flow through my life.

Faith comes to us as we hear the Word of God. The more we hear it, the more faith awakens within us. And there is a big difference between listening and hearing. Listening is simply the act of our ears picking up a signal. Hearing is when the signal transforms our heart. Listening is physical; hearing is spiritual.

Many people listen to the Word of God, but only a few hear the Word of God. When we hear the Word of God, it revolutionizes our entire outlook on life. Preacher Charles H. Spurgeon said, "A Bible that's falling apart usually belongs to someone who isn't." The Bible is more than just informational text; it's transformational living.

"The more we get into the Word of God, the more the Word of God gets into us."

Therefore it is vital that we immerse ourselves with God's Word. The more we get into the Word of God, the more the Word of God gets into us. In fact, it is impossible to fully know God without knowing His Word. If we genuinely want great faith, it takes great commitment to His Word. We must commit to seeking Him with all our hearts. This means hearing His Word, not just listening to it. Don't say God has been silent when your Bible has been closed. God's Word has everything you need for exactly what you're going through. It will raise your faith to where it needs to be.

By Asking

Luke 17:5 (NLV)
The followers said to the Lord, "Give us more faith."

It's appropriate to ask for more faith. In fact, we need to ask for more faith. The ancient statement from the Apostle James will stand true for all time:, "Ye have not, because ye ask not." God pours out an extra measure of faith for those who truly want it. God tends to meet us at our level of expectation. When you you ask for more faith expect for God to be faithful to grant you your request.

When you ask for faith, be willing to do whatever God says. God will not pour out more faith on you if you are not going to act on it. Asking God for faith is not just a request, it is an obedient act to do what He commands. Many people want to do what God wants them to do until they find out what He actually wants them to do. Faith will require you to do the most unlikely of things in the most unlikely of ways. Asking without obedience to act will clog the pipeline of God's provision.

Spend time asking God for faith every day. Ask with the intention and willingness to respond to whatever He says. Oswald Chambers said, "Faith is deliberate confidence in the character of God whose ways you may not understand at the time."

Never stop asking God for more. It's the people that "know it all" that think they don't need to ask for wisdom. But the greatest enemy of wisdom is pride; thinking you already know it all. Coach John Wooden said, "It's what you learn after you know it all that counts." Faith begins when pride ends. The future gets better when we allow our faith in God to guide us there. And always remember, where God guides, He always provides. If He has called us to it, He will see us through it. His promises stand true even when the circumstances are bleak. We just need faith for the journey.

REVIEW

KEYSTONE TRAIT 3

FAITH

(3.1) Get Faith

a) By Jesus
b) By Hearing
c) By Asking

3.2

Grow Faith

3.2

Grow Faith

Once we get faith, we are the ones responsible to grow it using the gifts God has given us. God gives us our gifts in the embryonic stage. It is up to us to water those seeds. No one can make you more creative, no one can make you a better thinker, no one can make you a better person. It's up to you to make it happen. Author James Allen said, "Men are anxious to improve their circumstances, but are unwilling to improve themselves; they therefore remain bound." You were created to take the seeds God has given you and grow them into great and mighty oaks of opportunity.

Growth doesn't happen automatically. It is a process built on deliberate effort and strategy. To grow your faith, you have to apply it to life's circumstances. You have to practice it in times of struggle. You have to choose to believe in something greater than you can see and then walk in it. Growing your faith requires an action plan.

Luke 2:52 (NIV)
And Jesus grew in wisdom and stature, and in favor with God and man.

Having an action plan to grow your faith will require work. You will never fully be used by God if you are unwilling to practice discipline. Jesus calls us to be disciples. In the Bible, the word disciple primarily refers to a student of Jesus. He is the Rabbi, meaning teacher, and we are His students. Think about what it truly means to be a student of Jesus. A student is striving to achieve something greater and is wholly focused on becoming an expert in that which they are studying. You cannot become a disciple without discipline; they are linked together as one in the same. In order to become a disciple, a student of Christ, it takes discipline. Johann Wolfgang von Goethe said, "Thinking is easy, acting is difficult, and to put one's thoughts into action is the most difficult thing in the world."

Here are three disciplines you need to grow your faith:

Get Resources

Abraham Lincoln said, "A capacity and taste for reading gives access to whatever has already been discovered by others."

No one will ever grow to their maximum potential without reading. Reading great books, stories, biographies, articles, and blogs pertaining to faith is one of the fastest ways to grow on your journey. Apply the wisdom and insights offered by others to your situation. Transform your mind by engaging with the great thoughts of others. If you could have spent a month with missionary and explorer David Livingston for $24.95, would you? If you could have spent a week with Billy Graham for $14.95, would you? If you could spend six months with your favorite Bible teacher for just $19.95, would you? You can, by reading their books! Fill your mind with their insights and resources, and grow your faith.

> "Books are to the mind what nutrition is to the body."

Books are to the mind what nutrition is to the body. The more you dive into great books, the more growth you'll experience. If you are pumping your life full of wisdom and inspiration, then you will overflow with those messages. We cannot give what we don't have. Reading is a way of inputting, so we can output. Learn from the mistakes and successes of others to help you accomplish more in your own life in less time. American philosopher Mortimer Jerome Adler said, "In the case of good books, the point is not how many of them you can get through, but rather how many can get through to you." If you want inspiration, simply read. If you want information, study what you read. If you want transformation, act on what you read.

2 Timothy 2:15 (KJV)
Study to shew thyself approved unto God, a workman that needeth not to be ashamed, rightly dividing the word of truth.

Get Mentors

Actor Will Rogers said, "A man only learns in two ways, one by reading, and the other by association with smarter people." Finding mentors who will lift you to a higher level is essential to your faith. I have heard that one good mentor can be more informative than a college education and more valuable than a decade's income.

Proverbs 13:20 (NIV)
Walk with the wise and become wise, for a companion of fools suffers harm.

We become like those we surround ourselves with. What kind of people are you surrounded by? One of the greatest traits of highly successful people is their drive to find and learn from those who excel in their field of interest. They intentionally seek to network with those who are further along on the journey, and they learn all they can from them.

We cannot reach our potential alone; we need others to help draw the best out of us. We were created for community. Sadly, trying to fly solo is the reason why so many people struggle to grow and succeed in their jobs, businesses, families, churches, ministries, etc… They can only expend so much personal effort and resources before they burn out. The way to impact the world is to work in community with those who share your passion or cause. A great place to begin is with a life coach who can help bring out the potential inside of you.

> "We cannot reach our potential alone; we need others to help draw the best out of us."

Proverbs 1:5 (NKJV)
A wise man will hear and increase learning, and a man of understanding will attain wise counsel,

Every great leader has a mentor to guide them and draw out the best in them. Luke had Yoda, Katniss had Haymitch, Frodo had Gandolph, Dorothy had Glenda, and the list goes on. Everyone should have a trusted coach to unleash their inner hero. In almost every profession, high capacity individuals use a coach: movie stars have acting coaches, singers have vocal coaches, and athletes have athletic coaches. Whether you are just starting out or are a seasoned professional, utilizing a coach is the best way to reach a higher level. In the same way, surround yourself with those who can speak wisdom into your life, and your faith will skyrocket to the top.

Get Experiences

All experiences are not created equal. Contrary to what you may have heard, experience is not the best teacher, educated experience is. There is a big difference between the two. Experience doesn't teach you anything unless you take the time to learn from it. It is not enough to simply go through a situation; you have to grow through it. We all know people who have gone through a lot but have learned nothing from it and show no change in their approach to life. Educating yourself as to what you have acquired through your experiences will give you incredible insight into the future. Speaker Tim Fargo said, "Analyze your mistakes. You've already paid the tuition, you might as well get the lesson."

It's not what we've experienced that shapes us; it's what we've learned from our experiences that truly shape us. Unless we take the time to reflect on our experiences, we are destined to repeat the past or worse, forget about it. One of my mentors, Dr. John C. Maxwell, says, "Reflective thinking turns experience into insight." Every experience brings with it a seed of success. Don't waste your experiences. Vernon Howard said, "Always walk through life as if you have something new to learn and you will." Keep yourself consistently curious, and you'll find yourself continuously courageous. Take time to sit down and learn from every experience, and you'll gain wisdom for a greater future. King Solomon, known as the wisest man in the Bible, wrote many wise sayings in the books of Proverbs and Ecclesiastes. God granted him wisdom because 1) he asked for it above all else, and 2) he committed himself to learning from his experiences. The following verse pretty much sums up his whole outlook on life; we would do well to adopt it for ours, as well:

Proverbs 24:32 (NIV)
I applied my heart to what I observed and learned a lesson from what I saw:

REVIEW

KEYSTONE TRAIT 3

FAITH

(3.1) Get Faith

a) By Jesus
b) By Hearing
c) By Asking

(3.2) Grow Faith

a) Get Resources
b) Get Mentors
c) Get Experiences

3.3

Give Faith

Faith

3.3

GIVE FAITH

Faith grows when it is given away. It says in the book of James that faith without works is dead. We shortchange ourselves and others when we don't live by faith. This means we walk in it and actively share it with others. It's great to receive something, but it's even greater to give something. Numerous studies have shown that helping others actually releases neurochemicals such as dopamine, serotonin, and oxytocin, which cause us to feel great. Psychology experts call this "helpers high." It is all rooted in the spiritual principle that what we make happen for others God makes happen for us.

Luke 6:38 (NIV)
Give, and it will be given to you. A good measure, pressed down, shaken together and running over, will be poured into your lap. For with the measure you use, it will be measured to you.

Look at that feedback loop of blessings! The more we help others, the more it helps us; and the more it helps us, the more we help others. It all starts with taking that first step to share your faith. The more you give, the more is given to you. American psychologist Dr. Karl Menninger was once asked, "What would you advise a person to do if he felt a nervous breakdown coming on?" Assuming he would expound on an intensive treatment plan, his response shocked them. He said, "Lock up your house, go across the railway tracks, find someone in need, and do something to help that person." When we take the focus off of ourselves and place it on another human being, we have a win-win situation. God is more concerned about our quality of giving than He is our quality of living. Out of our quality of giving, He will bless our quality of living.

Here are four ways you can share your faith:

By What You PRAY

Prayer builds our faith and effects change in others' lives. Jesus is our model for prayer. He separated Himself for times of prayer and intercession. Even now, He intercedes for us in Heaven.

Romans 8:34b (NIV)
Christ Jesus who died–more than that, who was raised to life — is at the right hand of God and is also interceding for us.

The Greek word for interceding here is entugchano, used to describe bringing a petition before a king on behalf of another person. What an amazing thought—Jesus is petitioning to His Father on our behalf. We should do no less for others. Ask for them, believe for them, and have faith for them. There is someone today who needs your prayers for tomorrow. Take the time to share your faith with them through intercession.

Prayer is powerful. It changes the climate of a situation. God hears our prayers and answers us. Archbishop and poet, Richard

Chenevix Trench, said, "We must not conceive of prayer as an overcoming God's reluctance, but as a laying hold of His highest willingness." Years ago, I came across this Scripture about the power of prayer:

Revelation 8:3-5 (NIV)
3 Another angel, who had a golden censer, came and stood at the altar. He was given much incense to offer, with the prayers of all God's people, on the golden altar in front of the throne.
4 The smoke of the incense, together with the prayers of God's people, went up before God from the angel's hand. 5 Then the angel took the censer, filled it with fire from the altar, and hurled it on the earth; and there came peals of thunder, rumblings, flashes of lightning and an earthquake.

Our prayers are like incense that rises to the Lord. The angel holds those prayers in a censer which he fills with fire from heaven, and then hurls it back to earth! KAPOW! Our prayers combined with God's holy fire = Holy Spirit power. Don't dismiss the significance of prayer in your own life as well as the lives of others.

By What You SAY

As with prayer, our words have tremendous power. God used words to create the universe; by them He spoke the world into existence.

Proverbs 18:21 (NIV)
"The tongue has the power of life and death..."

What a terrifying and amazing tool we have right in our mouths! Our tongues have the power of *life and death*. Nothing else in Scripture (apart from God Himself) has this kind of authority: not money, not our thoughts, not even our actions. We need to be very, *very* careful about the words we say.

> "Words are like seeds which will eventually produce sweet fruits or bitter roots."

With our words, we can elevate others' faith or annihilate it. Our words have creative and destructive power. Words always have consequences, whether good, bad, or indifferent. Words affect outcomes and create self-fulfilling prophecies. The impact of just one word can reverberate in the mind of another person for a lifetime. Think about how often you play back words in your head long after a conversation has ended. Author Napoleon Hill said, "Think twice before you speak, because your words and influence will plant the seed of either success or failure in the mind of another." Words are like seeds which will eventually produce sweet fruits or bitter roots. As faith givers, we must be very cautious and very intentional about the words we communicate.

Ephesians 4:29 (NIV)
Do not let any unwholesome talk come out of your mouths, but only what is helpful for building others up according to their needs, that it may benefit those who listen.

By What You Pay

Financially giving to others can open the door for faith to grow in their lives. I have experienced this firsthand. Years ago, my wife was on her way to church one Sunday when she felt prompted in her spirit to give money to a single father in our congregation. When she arrived at church, she sought me out before the service began and filled me in on this strong impression she felt. Familiar with the man she spoke of and aware of the long hours he worked just to pay the bills, I agreed. She asked me how much we should give, and I said, "I guess $100. Does that sound good?" to which she quickly responded, "That's what I felt like we should give him, too." She proceeded to grab an envelope, slide $100 into it, and then asked someone to give it to him anonymously on our behalf.

Here's where the story gets good. That same morning, this single father woke up feeling like he needed to give $100 to someone else in need at our church. He wrestled with the idea since he barely had enough to support his own family, and giving that large amount would deplete most of his money for the week. But he couldn't shake the urge to give the money away to this specific person. Taking a step of obedience and a leap of faith, he came to church and gave the money to the person, praying, "God, I trust you to provide."

I'm sure you can guess what happened. Right after he gave his money away, he anonymously received an envelope with exactly $100 in it. He couldn't believe it! As fast as he gave his money away, God showed up and replenished his resources. This experience raised his faith to a new level. He immediately came up and shared his story with the church that morning; he couldn't hold his gratitude in. My wife and I were blown away. He never knew the second hundred dollars came from us, but we got to see the hand of God at work through the whole process.

What you give could be the answer to someone's prayer. In doing so, you become the physical hands and feet of Jesus to show others God's provision for their situation. When you share your treasures, it raises the faith of others.

"When you share your treasures, it raises the faith of others."

Matthew 10:8b (NIV)
Freely you have received; freely give.

BY WHAT YOU PLAY

Get off the bleachers and get into the game of faith. We need to be in it to win it when it comes to making a difference. We weren't created to spectate; we were created to participate. You have been endowed with gifts and talents that are unique only to you. We impact people by being who we were designed to be. Someone, somewhere, needs you to do what God has specifically called you to do. Catherine of Siena said, "Be who God meant you to be and you will set the world on fire."

Luke 12:48 (NLT)
When someone has been given much, much will be required in return; and when someone has been entrusted with much, even more will be required.

When you use your gifts and talents, you will raise the faith of others. You may never know when or how, but be faithful to use them anyway. You never know which action today will change someone's tomorrow. Often, it is the smallest deeds that make the biggest difference in a person's life. Never underestimate your contribution.

The enemy always tries to belittle our gifts and talents. He tells us the lie that what we are doing doesn't matter. This is his way of getting us off our game. It's time to turn the tables and take charge! When you feel that you are less than God's best option for the opportunity before you, identify that as an attack from the enemy and a sure sign that you are right where God wants you to be. The enemy's lies are just blessings in disguise. Turn his attempts to dissuade you into fuel to propel you. Here's how Jesus described the devil:

John 8:44 (NIV)
He was a murderer from the beginning, not holding to the truth, for there is no truth in him. When he lies, he speaks his native language, for he is a liar and the father of lies.

Use your gifts and talents. Be who God created you to be. When you live in the fullness of who you are in Christ, you will always influence other people for the good of the Kingdom.

REVIEW

KEYSTONE TRAIT 3

FAITH

(3.1) Get Faith

a) By Jesus
b) By Hearing
c) By Asking

(3.2) Grow Faith

a) Get Resources
b) Get Mentors
c) Get Experiences

(3.3) Give Faith

a) By What You Pray
b) By What You Say
c) By What You Pay
d) By What You Play

Keystone Trait

1 Leadership

2 Intentionality

3 Faith

4 Enthusiasm

Keystone Trait

4

Enthusiasm

KEYSTONE TRAIT

4

ENTHUSIASM

"Success consists of going from failure to failure without loss of enthusiasm."
~ Winston Churchill

Have you ever seen something that just didn't make sense? How about finding two things that really don't go together? Here is a list of oxymorons (incongruous expressions) that I came across. How many do you use in your everyday conversation?

Found Missing
Same Difference
Threadless Screws
Jumbo Shrimp
Stand Down
Self-Help Group
Silent Alarm
Microsoft Works
Plastic Glasses
Tragic Comedy
Exact Estimate

Here are some phrases that really don't go together:

I cannot tolerate intolerance.
I'm sorry, but I never apologize.
Cheap is more expensive.
12-ounce pound cake
Click the start button, and shut down (for you Microsoft users).
Alone in a crowd.
Always remember you're unique…just like everyone else.

These phrases may sound contradictory, but there is nothing more contradicting than a grumpy Christian. Grumpy Christians are those who have lost their sense of gratitude. They have fixed their eyes on the temporal rather than the eternal. As followers of Christ, we are promised unconditional love from the Creator of the universe and an eternal hope. These two truths should override any lie of the enemy or earthly struggle we face.

1 Peter 1:3-6 (NIV)
3 Praise be to the God and Father of our Lord Jesus Christ! In
his great mercy he has given us new birth into a living hope
through the resurrection of Jesus Christ from the dead, 4 and
into an inheritance that can never perish, spoil or fade. This
inheritance is kept in heaven for you, 5 who through faith are
shielded by God's power until the coming of the salvation that
is ready to be revealed in the last time. 6 In all this you greatly
rejoice, though now for a little while you may have had to suffer
grief in all kinds of trials.

We have a living hope and an imperishable inheritance; God's power shields us. Knowing this, we should be the most enthusiastic people on the planet. The word "*enthusiasm*" comes from the Greek words *en*, meaning within or in, and *Theos*, meaning God. Enthusiasm comes from being "in God." When you are living fully "in God," joy becomes the anchor for your soul. Nineteenth-century English minister and professor Charles Kingsley said, "The men whom I have seen succeed best in life have always been cheerful and hopeful men, who went about their business with a smile on their faces, and took the changes and chances of this mortal life like men, facing rough and smooth alike as it came."

You can never choose all that happens *to* you, but you can always choose what happens *in* you. No one No one and nothing can make you miserable without your permission. As we discussed earlier, your outlook determines your attitude. Remember, S-T-R-E-S-S-E-D is just D-E-S-S-E-R-T-S spelled backward. Change your perspective and you can change your attitude. Stop complaining about what you don't have and start thanking God for what you do have. When you choose to acknowledge all the blessings God has given you, you will grow in gratitude and you will grow "in God." Start with the basics that apply to you: food to eat, a roof over your head, good health, loving relationships, a job, etc… Enthusiasm is the natural outflow of a grateful heart.

"Stop complaining about what you don't have and start thanking God for what you do have."

In contrast, the word "disease" comes from the Old French word *desaise*. The compound words are *des* meaning "without" and *aise* meaning "ease." Disease is defined as a state of disharmony because things are without ease. Many believers are spiritually diseased because of their negativity and ingratitude. Don't let conflicting, anxious thoughts steal your joy. Misery cannot manifest in a heart full of joy. Jesus came to bring us a joy that is literally out of this world.

John 10:10 (ESV)
The thief comes only to steal and kill and destroy. I came that they may have life and have it abundantly.

Jesus said He came to bring us abundant life. There is a big difference between just living and having abundant life. It's the difference between surviving and thriving. Which will you choose? Hellen Keller said, "Your success and happiness lies in you. Resolve to keep happy, and your joy and you shall form an invincible host against difficulties." Choosing to live with joy determines how successful your life will be. It takes 72 muscles to frown and only 23 to smile, which means you exert more energy being upset than you do choosing to be happy.

How do you maintain your enthusiasm in a world full of trials and tribulations? Let's look at three ways: Looking, Laughing, and Loving.

4.1

Always Looking

Enthusiasm

ALWAYS LOOKING

I want you to do an experiment with me…Are you ready? Follow these steps:

1) Take your hand a make a fist.
2) Put your thumb up like you're giving a "thumbs up" to someone with your thumbnail facing you.
3) Focus on your thumbnail only. Notice that everything else became blurry the moment you started to focus on your nail.
4) Now reverse the effect. Focus on an object behind your thumbnail in the room. Notice your thumbnail was the blurry object now.

What you focus on comes most clearly into view. The great part is that it's your choice: you get to decide whether you will focus on the good or the bad. I am reminded of Helen H. Lemmel's old hymn:

Turn your eyes upon Jesus
Look full in His wonderful face
And the things of earth will grow strangely dim
In the light of His glory and grace.

Your energy flows where your focus goes. This always happens to me when I am driving. If I look to the left, I start drifting left. If I look to the right, I start drifting right. If I don't stay focused and in my lane, I will inevitably end up wherever I am looking. It is the same spiritually. I must keep my eyes focused on God in order to live in the lane of His plan and not get distracted by what the world has to offer. When I veer out of His will, my life crashes.

Hebrews 12:1-3 (NIV)
1 Therefore, since we are surrounded by such a great cloud of witnesses, let us throw off everything that hinders and the sin that so easily entangles. And let us run with perseverance the race marked out for us, 2 fixing our eyes on Jesus, the pioneer and perfecter of faith. For the joy set before Him He endured the cross, scorning its shame, and sat down at the right hand of the throne of God. 3 Consider Him who endured such opposition from sinners, so that you will not grow weary and lose heart.

Proverbs 4:25-27 (NIV)
25 Let your eyes look straight ahead; fix your gaze directly before you. 26 Give careful thought to the paths for your feet and be steadfast in all your ways. 27 Do not turn to the right or the left; keep your foot from evil.

Notice these verses tell us to fix our eyes. The Greek word for fix is *aphoraó* meaning to turn our gaze away from everything else and place it on a singular object. We are instructed to turn our attention away from everything except Jesus. This means that we allow nothing to sidetrack us as we move toward

Him. We have to keep our focus, not allowing distractions to draw us in and derail our purpose.

A perfect example can be found in Homer's classic The Odyssey. In this tale, island creatures called Sirens lured sailors with their music and enchantment. While fixated on the Sirens, sailors would carelessly wreck their ships on the rocky coast, bringing about their destruction. We must keep our eyes on the prize and press on in our mission, or we will become like these sailors who lost sight of their mission.

There are five ways we can keep our eyes focused on the right things: Look Up, Look In, and Look Out.

Look Up

Psalm 121:1-2 (NIV)
1 I lift up my eyes to the mountains—where does my help come from? 2 My help comes from the Lord, the Maker of heaven and earth.

We are to lift our eyes up and focus on the Lord. The question we have to ask ourselves is, "Am I looking to God first when situations come up in my life?" Do we turn to Him immediately? Years ago, I heard a great statement: "Your reactions reveal more about you than your actions." If you really want to know if you are trusting God, when you are faced with something good or bad, see if He is your first thought. Do you praise Him for both the blessings and the pain? Is your reaction to life's challenges one of faith in God's promises? Our immediate reactions display the condition of our heart.

When we look to God, He gives us His perspective on the situation. Elevated to His vantage point, we can see things about our circumstances that we wouldn't otherwise be able to see. If you were to look ahead from where you stand now, your view would be blocked by various obstacles in front of you (i.e. trees, buildings, etc…). However, if you were to climb up a tree, you would have a bird's eye view above those obstacles. You would have a clearer perspective of the path ahead. Spiritually, we gain perspective by seeing life through the eyes of Christ. Our fears and doubts are eradicated when we see things as God sees them. As He says in the following passage, His ways are higher than ours, but we can ask for wisdom to see things as He does and to walk by faith in that knowledge.

Isaiah 55:9 (NIV)
As the heavens are higher than the earth, so are my ways higher than your ways and my thoughts than your thoughts.

God's ways are higher than our ways, and that is why He sometimes calls us to do things we don't always understand. We can only see the mountains and the valleys before us, but God sees the whole landscape. This is why we must be faithful to walk in the ways God has laid out for us, even when it looks impossible. Ask for His perspective and trust that He is faithful. When your faith is grounded in Christ, you can make godly choices and walk in them, because He is leading along the way.

LOOK IN

When we only focus on the problems around us we can easily miss the power within us. Thomas Edison once said, "If we did all the things we are capable of, we would literally astound ourselves." God has instilled within us a potential far beyond what we can fathom.

"When we only focus on the problems around us we can easily miss the power within us."

Ephesians 3:20-21 (NIV)
20 Now to Him who is able to do immeasurably more than all we ask or imagine, according to His power that is at work within us, 21 to Him be glory in the church and in Christ Jesus throughout all generations, forever and ever! Amen.

God's power is at work within us. What a promise we can hold on to! God is working in you to bring about something from you. Many people know who God is, but they don't know who they are in Christ. You are His masterpiece that He is continually working on until He brings you to completion in the end. We have to realize who we A.R.E. in Christ.

A–You are ACCEPTED

Romans 15:7 (NIV)
Accept one another, then, just as Christ accepted you, in order to bring praise to God.

You need to understand that God accepts you because of Jesus. When you place your faith in Jesus, God adopts you into His family. No longer do you have to feel abandoned or alone. Jesus loves you just as you are and welcomes you with open arms.

R–You are REDEEMED

Galatians 3:13 (NIV)

Christ redeemed us from the curse of the law by becoming a curse for us.

Not only does Christ accept you, but He also redeems you. Notice how the Scripture says He "redeemed us"—it's in the past tense. Your redemption was taken care of on the cross. He paid the full price for all of eternity. You don't have to earn salvation; it is not a process. Your faith in Christ offers you full and immediate redemption.

E–You Are EQUIPPED

Hebrews 13:21 (NIV)

May the God of peace, who through the blood of the eternal covenant brought back from the dead our Lord Jesus, that great Shepherd of the sheep, equip you with everything good for doing His will, and may He work in us what is pleasing to Him, through Jesus Christ, to whom be glory forever and ever. Amen.

Not only does Christ accept us and redeem us, but He also equips us with everything we need to fulfill all He has called us to. You are already fully equipped to do all that God has planned for you. Your job is to activate your faith by acknowledging the gifts and talents He has given you and stepping out to use them. The more you operate in your gifts, the greater your impact for the Kingdom will be.

LOOK OUT

Proverbs 12:26 (NIV)

The righteous choose their friends carefully, but the way of the wicked leads them astray.

“Show me your friends, and I’ll show you your future.” This old maxim still rings true today. Who we hang out with is who we will ultimately become like. Depending on which people you choose, this can be a good thing or a bad thing. English preacher Thomas Fuller said, “He's my friend that speaks well of me behind my back."

Moran Cerf, a neuroscientist at Northwestern University, has been studying decision-making for over a decade and has uncovered insightful research about the psychological effects of the company we keep. He states, “The more we study engagement, we see time and again that just being next to certain people actually aligns your brain with them. This means the people you hang out with actually have an impact on your engagement with reality beyond what you can explain. And one of the effects is you become alike.” This scientific discovery exposes a timeless truth about our circle of influence.

1 Corinthians 15:33 (NIV)

Do not be misled: "Bad company corrupts good character."

The good news is that we get to choose who we keep company with. We aren’t forced to have certain friends. But let’s make the distinction between friends and acquaintances. As followers of Christ, we are called to love everyone, but that does not mean we are called to be close friends with everyone. Jesus loved and interacted with anyone and everyone, but He shared close relationships with only a select few, His inner circle of friends, the 12 disciples. We are not called to isolate ourselves from people, but we do need to insulate ourselves from the wrong people. When we only focus on the problems around us we can easily miss the power within us. Associate with everyone, but only make an alliance with a few.

> "Associate with everyone, but only make an alliance with a few."

There are three kinds of people you will encounter in your life: Foes, Fans, and Friends. Foes think you are worse than you are, fans think you are better than you are, and friends know the truth about who you are.

Foes

Foes consider themselves your enemy. For whatever reason, they are out to take you down. Despite their opposition to us, we are still called to love our foes, but we don't need to invest our time and energy into winning them over or developing relationships with them. Usually, these are the people it is wise to insulate ourselves from, to avoid becoming combative, discouraged, or hurt. Foes are inevitable, especially to those living out their faith with enthusiasm. Aristotle said, "Criticism is something we can avoid easily by saying nothing, doing nothing, and being nothing."

Fans

These are your surface-level friends or groupies. They are the people who tell you what you want to hear instead of what you need to hear. Be careful of spending too much time with your fans because it is easy to become complacent and blind to weaknesses in your character. Fans are not all bad, though. They are the ones who will cheer you on and bring fun to the forefront. Just be aware that, even with their good intentions, they can still lead you astray.

FRIENDS

Friends are the chosen few people who will speak truth into your life through the good and bad seasons. Because they love you, they are committed to encouraging growth and refinement in your life. This means being honest with you about your weaknesses. Irish poet and playwright Oscar Wilde said, "True friends stab you in the front."

Proverbs 18:24 (NIV)
One who has unreliable friends soon comes to ruin, but there is a friend who sticks closer than a brother.

Jesus is the best friend you can have, and as Christians, we are called to be like Jesus. A Christ-like friend will stick closer than a brother. Your true friends are committed for the long haul, come what may. Challenges, sicknesses, losses—a great friend will be there through it all. Friends are a gift from God used to help us build community and sharpen each other. The quality of your friends determines the height of your success. Make sure you acquire a small group of Christ-centered friends who can speak truth and encouragement into your life, and you do the same for them.

Ecclesiastes 4:9-10 (NIV)
9 "Two are better than one, because they have a good return for their labor: 10 If either of them falls down, one can help the other up. But pity anyone who falls and has no one to help them up."

Look Back

Coach Lou Holtz said, "We aren't where we want to be; we aren't where we ought to be; but thank goodness we aren't where we used to be." It is when we look back that we see how far God has brought us. Too often we forget all that God has done for us. We allow our present circumstances to obscure our memories of His past faithfulness. Forgetting how God has provided for and protected us in the past is one way we lose sight of our faith. When challenges come, we need to remember that God came through for us before, and He can and will do it again.

I have been driving to my in-laws' house for almost 16 years now, but only recently have I managed to get there on my own. They live in the country on the backroads, and every time we drive there, I am talking, thinking, or listening. I've always just relied on my wife to tell me each and every turn (and there are a lot). Left to myself, I always forgot which way to go. So, the first time I made it to their house without having to ask for directions, I was quite pleased with myself.

In the same way I repeatedly forgot the directions to my in-laws' house, so too can we forget God's directions to us in the past and find ourselves in danger of making a wrong turn. The Bible encourages us always to remember and speak of His past faithfulness. Why? So that we never forget how amazing our God was, is, and will always be! I have heard it said, "Don't remember what you should forget...and don't forget what you should remember." In the Old Testament, the Israelites set up memorial stones at certain locations to help them remember what the Lord had done in that place. We too need to create reminders for ourselves, lest we forget God's gracious provision.

Joshua 4:20-24 (NIV)

20 And Joshua set up at Gilgal the twelve stones they had taken out of the Jordan. 21 He said to the Israelites, "In the future when your descendants ask their parents, 'What do these stones mean?' 22 tell them, 'Israel crossed the Jordan on dry ground.' 23 For the Lord your God dried up the Jordan before you until you had crossed over. The Lord your God did to the Jordan what he had done to the Red Sea when he dried it up before us until we had crossed over. 24 He did this so that all the peoples of the earth might know that the hand of the Lord is powerful and so that you might always fear the Lord your God."

DON'T LOOK DOWN

Psalm 3:3 (NIV)

But you, LORD, are a shield around me, my glory, the One who lifts my head high.

> "We are no longer victims, but victors in Christ!"

We don't have to look down in despair or defeat because we serve a God who lifts our head. He promises to never leave us nor forsake us. Jesus said, "In this world you will have trouble. But take heart! I have overcome the world." We are no longer victims, but victors in Christ! It was only when Peter looked down at the waves beneath his feet that he started to falter. When he kept his eyes on Jesus, he could walk on water. Just like in the movies when two characters are doing something adventurous, such as scaling a skyscraper, and one says to the other, "Whatever you do… don't look down," we too need to keep our focus forward on the task ahead, looking to the One who goes before us.

If I were to ask you to walk across an eight-foot beam that was only two feet off the ground, would you do it? Probably. There isn't much risk in that. What if I raised it five feet off the ground? Most likely. But, what if I raised it 25 feet off the ground, or even 50 feet? How about 500 feet or 5,000 feet? At what point did you drop out and why? Was it because you didn't know how to walk across an eight-foot beam? Of course not. It takes the same level of skill to walk across an eight-foot beam at 500 feet as it does at two feet off the ground. In reality, nothing changed except for your increasing fear of failure. Fear keeps us from going higher and believing God for greater opportunities. Look up for perspective, look within for courage, look out for opportunities, look back in remembrance, but whatever you do…don't look down!

Philippines 3:12-14 (NIV)
12 Not that I have already obtained all this, or have already arrived at my goal, but I press on to take hold of that for which Christ Jesus took hold of me. 13 Brothers and sisters, I do not consider myself yet to have taken hold of it. But one thing I do: Forgetting what is behind and straining toward what is ahead, 14 I press on toward the goal to win the prize for which God has called me heavenward in Christ Jesus.

Review

Keystone Trait 3

Enthusiasm

(4.1) Looking

a) Look Up
b) Look In
c) Look Out
- Foes
- Fans
- Friends

d) Look Back
e) Don't Look Down

4.2

Always Laughing

Enthusiasm

4.2

ALWAYS LAUGHING

You'll never live life to the fullest if you can't laugh. Holocaust survivor and founder of Logotherapy Viktor Frankel said, "Humor, more than anything else in the human make-up, can afford an aloofness and an ability to rise above any situation, if only for a few seconds."

Proverbs 17:22 (NIV)
A cheerful heart is good medicine, but a crushed spirit dries up the bones.

Laughter is a natural medicine that heals the soul. God designed us with a physiological response to joy. When we smile and laugh, the brain releases dopamine, a powerful neurotransmitter that produces feelings of happiness. It has also been proven to boost the immune system as well as lower blood pressure and increase oxygen intake. We are hard-wired with an internal happiness mechanism that is triggered by a joyful attitude. Numerous studies have discovered that happy people live much healthier lives. It makes sense that, as followers of Christ, we should have the most reasons to laugh and experience joy. We should be the most joyous people in the world.

Nehemiah 8:10b (NIV)
"Do not grieve, for the joy of the LORD is your strength."

We must be intentional about laughter and make it part of our everyday experience. Ralph Waldo Emerson said, "For every minute you are angry you lose sixty seconds of happiness."

Another expression of joy is delight. Delight comes from the Latin word meaning "to allure." What is more alluring than someone who is delighted or full of joy? Joy is an antidote for stress, anxiety, and fear. These are heavy loads to carry, but delight in its very essence is a lightness of being. Our greatest delight comes from the Lord and what He has done for us. Living in Christ is where we find the fullness of joy. When we live *in* Christ, we are in relationship with Him, as opposed to living *for* Him, which feels more like dutiful service. C.S. Lewis said, "God cannot give us a happiness and peace apart from Himself, because it is not there. There is no such thing."

Here are some tips to stay full of joy.

Laugh In Your Busyness

When life gets busy and stressful, often the first thing to go is laughter. Before long, we realize we haven't LOL'd (Laughed Out Loud) in a long time. This not only has physiological repercussions, including: heart problems, depression, high-blood pressure, lowered immunity, but it also affects us spiritually. We need to incorporate laughter into our lives. All work plus no play equals spiritual disarray.

> "All work plus no play equals spiritual disarray."

Our lives were designed to move in rhythm. God ordained the Sabbath to keep us in rhythm. When we violate His ordinance, we suffer the consequence of an overstocked and underfulfilled life. The Sabbath keeps us in a perfect oscillation of work and rest. It is the same with all of nature. Think about it: the seasons are designed to flow from the barrenness of winter to new life in spring and the full bloom of summer, followed by the harvest of fall. Each day has a rhythm of light and dark; our bodies need to work and rest. In all things, we find the oscillating rhythm of life.

The purpose of the Sabbath (and I am not here to debate whether it should be a specific day or simply a principle to live by) is to establish and maintain that rhythm. God modeled it for us in the Creation story. We take part in the Sabbath to rest and give God honor, to refrain from overworking and under-worshiping. We can also experience mini-Sabbaths as we take time to pause and laugh throughout the week. Laughter lifts the spirit and refuels our energy tanks. We need to rest in order to be our best.

Psalm 23:1-3 (NIV)
1 The Lord is my shepherd, I lack nothing. 2 He makes me lie down in green pastures, He leads me beside quiet waters, 3 He refreshes my soul. He guides me along the right paths for His name's sake.

Making time to step away from the demands of work to laugh and enjoy life can do wonders for your spiritual well-being. When we are trapped under the burden of life's pressures, it is difficult, if not impossible, to experience joy. The longer we go forsaking the delight of laughter, the more burned out we will get. I like how Will Rogers put it: "If you find yourself in a hole, the first thing to do is stop digging." Some people don't just worry occasionally, they worry recreationally. Don't make life harder than it has to be. Find ways to simplify your schedule and create margin for fun. Don't get so busy you forget how to laugh.

Look over your schedule. Are you too busy? Do you feel exhausted, burned out, grumpy? Schedule some downtime by blocking it off on your calendar. Whether it is a couple of hours to watch a funny movie with your family or meet for coffee with a friend, or a weekend getaway to refresh your soul, create space for joy and rest to enter your life again.

Laugh At Yourself

William Arthur Ward said, "To make mistakes is human; to stumble is commonplace; to be able to laugh at yourself is maturity."

Proverbs 29:11 (NIV)
Fools give full vent to their rage, but the wise bring calm in the end.

You are going to mess up. That's right, so you might as well just accept it. If you expect perfection and take yourself too seriously all the time, you will end up a disillusioned, bitter person. Lighten up and learn how to laugh at your mistakes and faults. I'm not saying that you shouldn't strive for excellence, but don't let past mistakes destroy your joy. If you can't laugh at your own shortcomings, you will find it difficult to find grace for the shortcomings of others. You are going to let yourself down, and so will others. Without the joy of humor, not only will you be miserable, you will make others feel miserable, too.

Most people have the wrong perception of failure. They see it as something to be avoided rather than something to be leveraged. The truth is failure can bring us one step closer to success. Robert Kennedy said, "Only those who dare to fail greatly can ever achieve greatly." My mentor, Dr. John C. Maxwell taught me early on that if you aren't making any mistakes, it's a sure sign you're playing it too safe. I realized that you have to risk big in order to receive big. Failure is an essential component to success. It is the learning process that takes you from average to great. We should never intentionally try to fail, but we must learn how to embrace the lessons failure has to teach us.

Proverbs 24:16 (NIV)
For though the righteous fall seven times, they rise again, but the wicked stumble when calamity strikes.

Those who are able to gracefully recover from their mistakes will proceed successfully toward their goals. When we beat ourselves up over our mistakes, we open the door to discouragement. And discouragement literally "disses" our courage to move forward. Part of stepping out in faith is having the courage to fail. Fearing failure is an obstacle to faith. God's grace is bigger than

"Part of stepping out in faith is having the courage to fail."

your biggest failures. Instead of dwelling on your mistakes, laugh at them and learn from them. Vaclav Havel, former President of the Czech Republic, said, "Anyone who takes himself too seriously always runs the risk of looking ridiculous; anyone who can consistently laugh at himself does not."

Laugh Through Your Circumstances

1 Thessalonians 5:16-18 (NIV)
16 Rejoice always, 17 pray continually, 18 give thanks in all circumstances; for this is God's will for you in Christ Jesus.

Notice that we are called to give thanks in all circumstances; it is God's will for us. We are not called to give thanks *for* our circumstances, but to give thanks *in* them. Those who can remain grateful in the midst of difficult conditions are the ones who know true joy. There is purpose in the pain; God is working all things for our good. He knows the big picture; we are called to trust Him. It's not that we want tough circumstances, but we can learn to give thanks for them.

When we feel we deserve more than we currently have or are getting, it breeds discontentment and ungratefulness in us, which then turns to selfishness and pride. Pride keeps us from our fullest potential. Having an attitude of gratitude ensures we are on the road to success. Circumstances change; we will experience the heights and the depths, but we are called to stay humble through them all. We can't control *what* we go through, but we can control *how* we go through it. The difference be-

> "We can't control what we go through, but we can control how we go through it."

tween successful people and unsuccessful people is their response to circumstances. American novelist Raymond Chandler said, "Ability is what you're capable of doing. Motivation determines what you do. Attitude determines how well you do it."

Proverbs 15:13 (NIV)
A happy heart makes the face cheerful, but heartache crushes the spirit.

Helen Keller said, "Keep your face to the sunshine and you cannot see a shadow." Remain steadfast in your thinking and be on guard at all times. Focus on faith-filled thoughts instead of your feelings. "Fake it 'til you make it" is a popular expression to live by. We may not feel joyful, but if we practice joy and meditate on joy, eventually we will feel it, too. Develop faith-filled habits each day. Choose to laugh, even when you don't feel like it. No one ever suffered from a cheerful heart.

Look up five verses on the joy of the Lord, and write them down on a notecard. Carry it with you and repeat the verses throughout the day, until you have them committed to memory. When tempted to despair or be angry, pull out your card and remind yourself to live with joy instead.

Proverbs 15:15 (NIV)
All the days of the oppressed are wretched, but the cheerful heart has a continual feast.

REVIEW

KEYSTONE TRAIT 3

ENTHUSIASM

(4.1) Always Looking

a) Look Up
b) Look In
c) Look Out
- Foes
- Fans
- Friends

d) Look Back
e) Don't Look Down

(4.2) Always Laughing

a) Laugh In Your Busyness
b) Laugh At Yourself
c) Laugh Through Your Circumstances

4.3

Always Loving

Enthusiasm

Always Loving

Mother Teresa said, "Spread love everywhere you go. Let no one ever come to you without leaving happier."

Composers, Hal David and Burt Bacharach, were on to something back in 1965 when they wrote…"What the world needs now is love, sweet love." If there is one word that should define Christians, it is undoubtedly LOVE.

1 John 4:8 (NIV)
Whoever does not love does not know God, because God is love.

All of Scripture revolves around the central idea of love because that is who He is. Love is what defined Christ and love is what should define us as His disciples. Though David's and Bacharach's song stands the test of time, they weren't the first to remind us that what the world needs now is love. The Apostle Paul could have had a hit song when he penned this:

1 Corinthians 13:13 (NIV)
And now these three remain: faith, hope, and love. But the greatest of these is love.

More than faith or hope, love is considered the greatest spiritual attribute. Why? God defines us by who we are in Him, but the world defines us by what we do. Faith and hope are internal qualities, but love is the external expression of what is in our hearts. We show the world who God is by how we love them.

1 Samuel 16:7b (NIV)
The LORD does not look at the things people look at. People look at the outward appearance, but the LORD looks at the heart.

We are God's representatives of love to the world. Martin Luther King Jr said, "People are often led to causes and often become committed to great ideas through persons who personify those ideas. They have to find the embodiment of the idea in flesh and blood in order to commit themselves to it." In order to spread the cause of Christ, we must remain in Him and become like Him in word and deed.

John 15:9-12 (NIV)
9 As the Father has loved me, so have I loved you. Now remain in my love. 10 If you keep my commands, you will remain in my love, just as I have kept my Father's commands and remain in His love. 11 I have told you this so that my joy may be in you and that your joy may be complete. 12 My command is this: Love each other as I have loved you.

What a great responsibility we have been given! God is love, and we are commissioned to display that love toward each other as believers so that peo-

> "People should see Christ when they see us."

ple will be drawn to Christ when they look at our lives. People should see Christ when they see us.

In the 1950s, a skinny preacher named David Wilkerson infiltrated a gang-controlled neighborhood on the streets of New York, preaching the Gospel. One of the most notorious and most feared gang leaders, Nicky Cruz, approached the preacher one frightful day and said, "You come near me, and I'll kill you!"

Wilkerson replied, "Yeah, you could do that. You could cut me up into a thousand pieces and lay them in the street, and every piece will still love you."

Cruz later miraculously gave his life to the Lord, transforming him from the inside out. Wilkerson wrote about it in one of the most famous Christian books of all time, *The Cross and the Switchblade*.

What an incredible response to a life-threatening encounter! Wilkerson was committed to loving Cruz even if he was brutally killed in the process. How committed are we to loving others, no matter how much they hate us or irritate us? Wilkerson's response challenges my faith…a lot! I confess, it isn't always easy to show love even to those I do love; loving strangers and enemies is infinitely harder. To live like Jesus means to love like Jesus, with humility and compassion, the way Wilkerson did.

Before He died on the cross for us, Jesus prayed that we would love like He did. Jesus equates our love for others to our love for Him. If you truly love God you will truly love others.

Matthew 25:40 (NIV)
The King will reply, "Truly I tell you, whatever you did for one of the least of these brothers and sisters of mine, you did for me."

What does love look like? Using the word LOVE as an acronym, let's look at four ways love is expressed.

L = LISTENING

One way you can show love for others is by listening to them. The more you listen to another person, the more they feel loved by you. President Theodore Roosevelt is credited with saying, "No one cares how much you know until they know how much you care." When others believe they have a voice, they feel they have a place.

James 1:19 (NIV)
My dear brothers and sisters, take note of this: Everyone should be quick to listen, slow to speak and slow to become angry...

It's been said that God gave us two ears and one mouth for a reason: to listen twice as much as we talk. A person will never gain the respect of others if they cannot listen. Listening is more than just hearing, though. Hearing is the physical act of gathering information through the ears. Listening is the mental processing and emotional understanding of the information we take in. To listen well, you must be fully present in the moment, absorbing both the verbal and nonverbal cues of the person before you. Listening is the awareness of body language, tone, eye contact, and the conceptual context accompanying what is being said. Listening this way, you can truly know the heart of the person speaking to you. Businessman Peter Drucker, said, "The most important thing in communication is to hear what isn't being said."

Everyone has a story that deserves to be heard. We are all on a journey, and we are called to connect with each other and encourage each other along life's path. People are not a means to an end, a checkbox on your religious agenda. Love others by listening intently and genuinely caring for them. In doing so, you will earn the privilege to speak truth and love into their lives.

"If you truly want to show someone how much you care, listen to what they say."

Proverbs 18:13 (NIV)
To answer before listening—that is folly and shame.

O = OPTIMISM

The Bible says the Lord loves a cheerful giver. Giving of your time, talents, and treasures to serve others with a cheerful and optimistic heart is another way to show love. Author Gordon MacDonald said, "You can tell whether you are becoming a servant by how you act when you're treated like one." The way you serve reveals what's in your heart. When you truly love others, you will be excited to serve them. Granted, people aren't always easy to serve (just ask any waitress), but as Christians, we are called to do our work as unto the Lord. Remember Who it is that you are truly serving, and do so with a heart full of love and good cheer.

Proverbs 11:25 (NIV)
A generous person will prosper; whoever refreshes others will be refreshed.

When we serve others with enthusiasm, we lift their spirits. You get to give a blessing and be a blessing. No one wants to feel like a burden. Nothing is worse than someone who serves grudgingly, with a frown or scowl on their face. Serving is not a burden; it is a privilege. Jesus was never frustrated by the needs of others; He served without reservation, sacrificing His own comfort and ease for the healing of others. We should serve in the same way, with even greater enthusiasm for all He has done for us.

> "Serving is not a burden; it is a privilege."

Philippians 2:5-8 (NIV)
5 In your relationships with one another, have the same mindset as Christ Jesus: 6 Who, being in very nature God, did not consider equality with God something to be used to his own advantage; 7 rather, he made himself nothing by taking the very nature of a servant, being made in human likeness. 8 And being found in appearance as a man, he humbled himself by becoming obedient to death—even death on a cross!

V = VOLUNTEERING

Raise a hand. Step forward. Volunteer yourself. Take the initiative to show love. You can't truly love others while looking to be loved. It must come from a place of selfless ambition. Pour yourself out, not expecting anything in return. This is unconditional love. It's not a matter or manipulation or recognition. A volunteer, by its definition, is someone who does some act or enters into a transaction without being under any legal obligation to do so, and without being promised any remuneration for his services. John Bunyan said, "You have not lived today unless you've done something for someone who can never repay you."

Choosing to give of your life when it is not required of you is the purest form of love. People's lives are transformed by unconditional love. Once we stop asking, "What can I get?" and start asking, "What can I give?" we will experience the joy of making a difference. When James Calvert ventured out as a missionary to the cannibals of the Fiji Islands, the ship's captain tried to turn him back saying, "You will lose your life and the lives of those with you if you go among such savages." To that Calvert replied, "We died before we came here." Volunteering your love is about sacrificing your comfort for the greater good.

Luke 9:24 (NIV)
For whoever wants to save their life will lose it, but whoever loses their life for me will save it.

E = ENDURANCE

Servanthood is a not a one-time event; it's a life-long endeavor of valuing people that requires faithful endurance. It is the ultimate expression of a caffeinated Christian adventure. Don't stop serving. I have met many decaf Christians who feel they have "paid their dues" and no longer need to serve. They think they've somehow grown out of the servant role. But you never move beyond being a servant no matter who you may be. It is not something you do for a season and then graduate from. Don't grow weary from serving. Yes, it is hard work to love and serve others. It requires our blood, sweat, and tears, but the Bible urges us not to grow weary in doing good. Don't give up because it's hard or because you feel like you deserve some kind of prize for your efforts. The payoff from serving far outweighs the comfort of sitting. Humble yourself; surrender your selfishness and pride for love's reward. There may be those who take advantage of us, but it is always better to serve others than to serve ourselves. When we are in God's will, the more we pour out, the more He pours in. Let me remind you once more of this verse:

> "The payoff from serving far outweighs the comfort of sitting."

Hebrews 12:1-3 (NIV)

1 Therefore, since we are surrounded by such a great cloud of witnesses, let us throw off everything that hinders and the sin that so easily entangles. And let us run with perseverance the race marked out for us, 2 fixing our eyes on Jesus, the pioneer and perfecter of faith. For the joy set before Him he endured the cross, scorning its shame, and sat down at the right hand of the throne of God. 3 Consider him who endured such opposition from sinners, so that you will not grow weary and lose heart.

Don't lose heart. Keep loving. Keep serving. Keep looking up. This is Kingdom work we are about, and He deserves our very best. Arthur Ashe said, "True heroism is remarkably sober, very undramatic. It is not the urge to surpass all others at whatever cost, but the urge to serve others at whatever cost."

REVIEW

KEYSTONE TRAIT 3

ENTHUSIASM

(4.1) Always Looking

a) Look Up
b) Look In
c) Look Out
- Foes
- Fans
- Friends

d) Look Back
e) Don't Look Down

(4.2) Always Laughing

a) Laugh In Your Busyness
b) Laugh At Yourself
c) Laugh Through Your Circumstances

(4.3) Always Loving

a) Listening
b) Optimism
c) Volunteering
d) Endurance

CONCLUSION

Leadership, intentionality, faith, and enthusiasm are the four keystone traits required to live an abundant life. It's simple, just not easy. But if we can harness them we can fulfill our God-given potential.

I hope you received what you needed from this book. My prayer is that you do something with it. It's one thing to know what you need to do, it's a whole other thing to actually do what you need to do. Let me encourage you to keep challenging yourself to get better at this thing called life. Remember, life is like a bank account, you can only get out of it what you have put into it. Great withdraws can't happen unless you've made even greater deposits. Only when we take the time to reflect and work on ourselves do we really improve. Reflective thinking opens the door for future possibilities. Greek philosopher Socrates observed, "The unexamined life is not worth living."

Start examining yourself by taking the challenge below…

Rate yourself on a scale from 1-10 (10 being the highest, 1 being the lowest) on how well you are doing in the four keystone traits of L.I.F.E.

(Circle your rating)
Leadership...1 2 3 4 5 6 7 8 9 10

Intentionality...1 2 3 4 5 6 7 8 9 10

Faith...1 2 3 4 5 6 7 8 9 10

Enthusiasm...1 2 3 4 5 6 7 8 9 10

Think through 2-3 things you need to do in order to raise your score from where it is to a higher level for each of the four areas. Commit to these strategies as you do your best to fulfill them. I have also added a few basic quick examples to help kickstart some ideas.

Leadership
1)____

____

2)____

____

3)____

____

Examples:
- *Create a declaration list of who you are in Christ and read it out loud to yourself every morning for a month.*
- *Write a purpose statement for each major area of your life... personal...family...work...etc.*

Intentionality

1)____

____

2)____

____

3)____

____

Examples:

- *Think through 3 major goals you want to accomplish over the next few months.*
- *Do something impactful that you have always feared to do in order to overcome it and make a difference.*

Faith

1)____

____

2)____

____

3)____

____

Examples:

- *Create a growth plan for your spiritual well-being involving books, mentors, experiences you want to accomplish.*
- *Make a list of people you are going to pray for each day.*

Enthusiasm

1)____

____

2)____

____

3)____

____

Examples:

- *Schedule a personal retreat in the next month so you can laugh and refresh.*
- *Start volunteering in a ministry based opportunity in order to show the love of Christ.*

ABOUT THE AUTHOR

John is a gifted speaker, author, blogger, musician, artist, life, coach, leadership coach, and business coach. He has been studying, living, and teaching about faith, leadership, and innovation for over 18 years. John has been personally mentored by Dr. John C. Maxwell and serves as a certified coach/speaker/trainer for the John Maxwell Team. He has served in full-time pastoral roles at small and large size churches all across the country while speaking and coaching in the business community. He has a passion to help people determine their purpose, develop their potential, and do great things. He and his wife live with their 3 children in Southern Indiana where he is currently serving as Associate Pastor. You can find more about John Barrett and his resources by visiting www.johnbarrettblog.com.

BOOK ME TO SPEAK AT YOUR
NEXT EVENT...

JohnBarrettLeadership.com

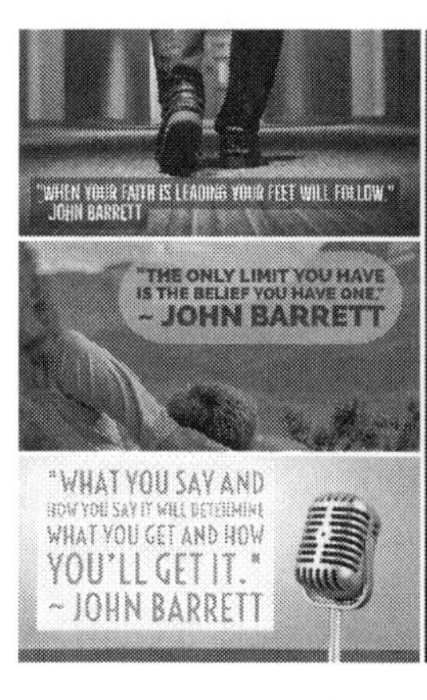

"WHEN YOUR FAITH IS LEADING YOUR FEET WILL FOLLOW."
JOHN BARRETT
"THE ONLY LIMIT YOU HAVE IS THE BELIEF YOU HAVE ONE."
~ JOHN BARRETT
"WHAT YOU SAY AND HOW YOU SAY IT WILL DETERMINE WHAT YOU GET AND HOW YOU'LL GET IT."
~ JOHN BARRETT
50 POWERFUL QUOTES TO TAKE YOU SOMEWHERE BETTER
John Barrett
FREE EBOOK OF 50 POWERFUL QUOTES AVAILABLE AT
WWW.JOHNBARRETTLEADERSHIP.COM
JUST FOR YOU

Leadology
John Barrett
Do You Want to
Level Up
YOUR
Leadership
Ability?
THIS BOOK SHOWS YOU HOW
Leadology Available At:
amazon
iBooks
JohnBarrettLeadership.com

John Barrett
Don't Get Stuck
Weekly Inspiration
Designed To Maximize Your Leadership
www.JohnBarrettLeadership.com
New Content Every Tuesday

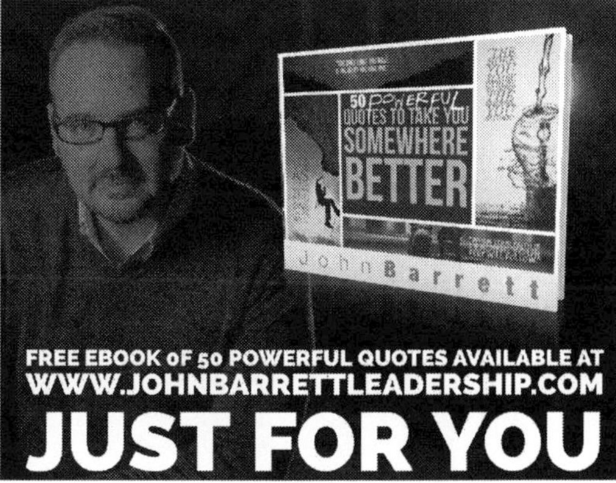

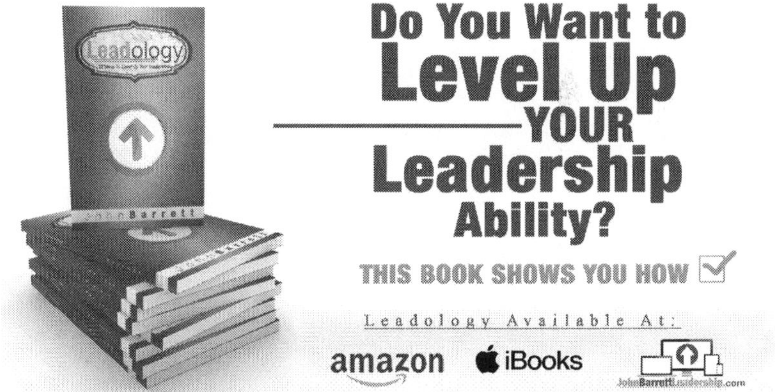

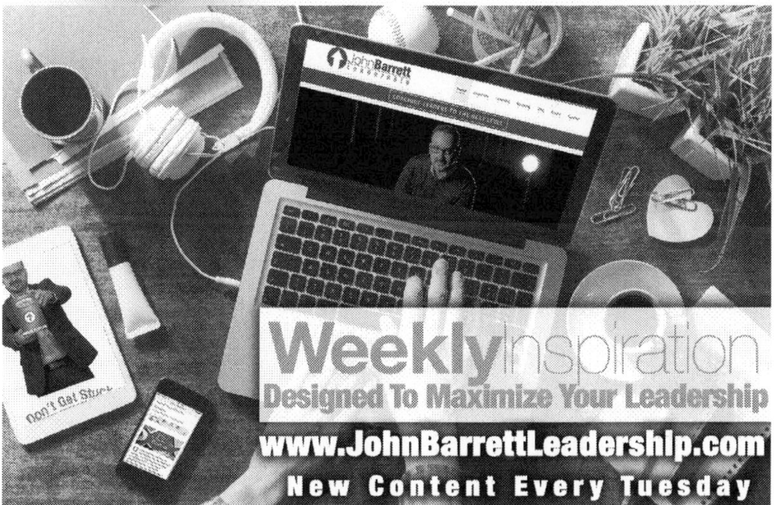

The Worship Revolution

Amazon | iBooks | Kindle

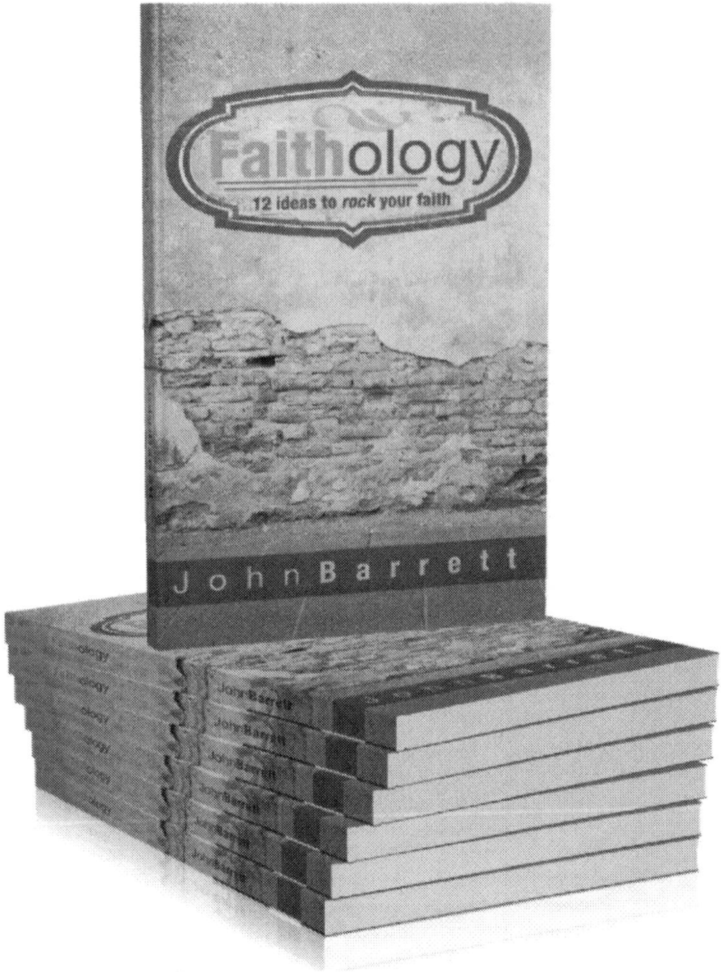
Faithology
12 ideas to rock your faith
John Barrett

Made in the USA
Middletown, DE
15 February 2019